Essentials

of health and safety at work

© Crown copyright 2006

First published 1988
Second edition 1990
Third edition 1994
Fourth edition 2006

ISBN 0 7176 6179 2

Applications for reproduction should be made in writing to:
Licensing Division, Her Majesty's Stationery Office,
St Clements House, 2-16 Colegate, Norwich NR3 1BQ
or by e-mail to hmsolicensing@cabinet-office.x.gsi.gov.uk

Acknowledgements
Bentley Motors Ltd
Greencore Group plc
Kajima Construction Europe (UK) Ltd
Science Photo Library
United Utilities

Contents

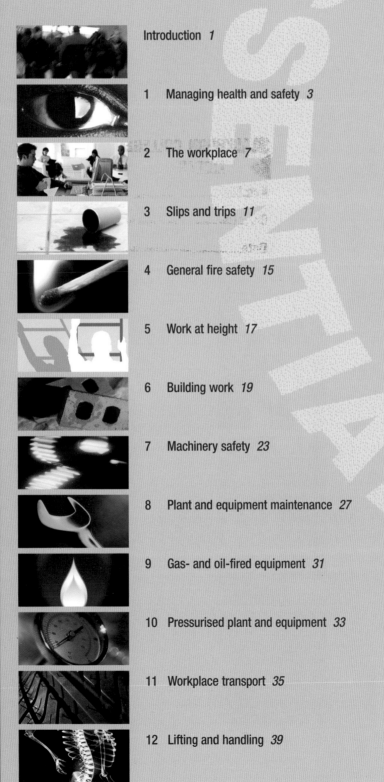
HSE Infoline 0845 345 0055   HSE website www.hse.gov.uk   HSE Books 01787 881165

Contents

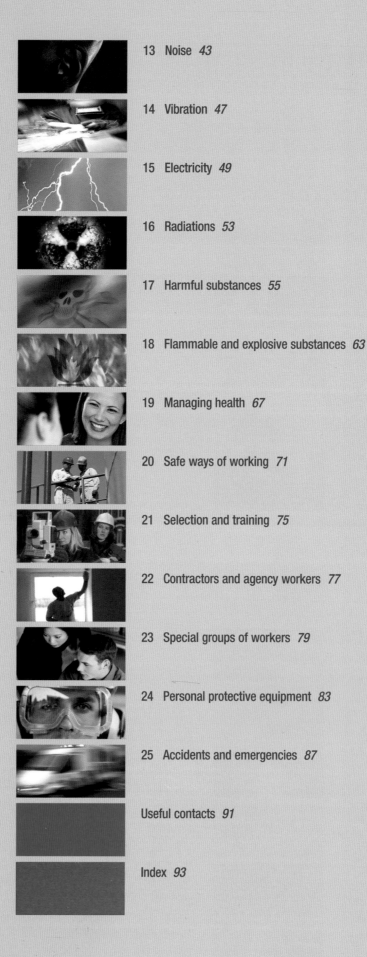

HSE Infoline 0845 345 0055   HSE website www.hse.gov.uk   HSE Books 01787 881165

Introduction

Why read this book?

Health and safety management should be a straightforward part of managing your business as a whole. It involves practical steps that protect people from harm and at the same time protect the future success of your business.

There are legal health and safety requirements that you have to meet, but accidents also cost money and time – people off work, material costs and damage to buildings, plant or product. These costs are often not covered by insurance.

This book explains what the law requires and helps you put it into practice.

What are the main causes of ill health and accidents at work?

Every year over 200 people are killed at work and several hundred thousand more are injured and suffer ill health.

The biggest causes of days off work sick are aches and pains such as back problems (see Chapter 12) and stress (see Chapter 19).

The most common causes of serious accidental injury at work are slips and trips (see Chapter 3).

The most common causes of death from accidents are falls from a height (see Chapter 5) and being struck by vehicles in the workplace (see Chapter 11).

The law and guidance

There are two main kinds of health and safety law. Some is very specific about what you must do, but some, such as the Health and Safety at Work etc Act 1974 (HSW Act), is general, requiring you to do what is 'reasonably practicable' to ensure health and safety. The Health and Safety Executive (HSE) has produced publications (many available to view at www.hse.gov.uk) to help you to decide what this means in practice.

Information about useful publications and websites is given in a 'Find out more' section in each chapter. Priced publications have an ISBN number. HSE leaflets are free for a single copy, but are sold in priced packs for multiple copies.

Introduction

This book

Chapter 1 suggests how you can tackle the basics of health and safety. It tells you how to identify, assess and control the activities that might cause harm in your business.

Chapters 2 to 25 are for anyone who needs to know more about a particular subject. Each chapter tells you what you need to do to work safely as well as what laws apply.

Looking at your business in the way this book suggests will help you stay safe. It will go a long way to satisfying the law – including the risk assessment that you must do under the Management of Health and Safety at Work Regulations 1999. It might save you money as well!

HSE Infoline 0845 345 0055 HSE website www.hse.gov.uk HSE Books 01787 881165

Managing health and safety

The hazards

- **A hazard** is anything that might cause harm (eg chemicals, electricity, vehicles, working from ladders).
- **Risk** is the chance (big or small) of harm being done, as well as how serious that harm could be.

Who do I have to consider?

You need to consider people who:

- work for you, including casual workers, part-timers, trainees and subcontractors;
- use workplaces you provide;
- are allowed to use your equipment;
- visit your premises;
- may be affected by your work, eg your neighbours or the public;
- use products you make, supply or import; or
- use your professional services, eg if you are a designer.

How to manage health and safety

What you have to do to manage health and safety effectively is:

- Know about the risks in your work.
- Control the risks that need it.
- Make sure the risks stay controlled.

Know about the risks in your work

Risk is a part of everyday life, and even quite straightforward businesses can have a range of 'hazards'. You are not expected to eliminate all risk. What you must do is make sure you know about the main risks that affect you, and what you need to do to manage them responsibly.

Thinking this through is called 'risk assessment'. All businesses have to do this by law. It's also practical, as you can make sure you put effort into the right things, avoid wasting time on trivial risks, and don't miss anything important.

How to assess risks

Look for all the 'hazards' in your work, considering what could realistically harm people. For each of these hazards think:

- How serious could the harm be? Is it a cut finger or months off work with a back injury?
- Who could be harmed, and how likely is that?
- Do you need to do more to control the risks?

The law

Under the Health and Safety at Work etc Act 1974 (the HSW Act), you have to ensure the health and safety of yourself and others who may be affected by what you do or do not do. It applies to all work activities and premises and everyone at work has responsibilities under it, including the self-employed.

The Management of Health and Safety at Work Regulations 1999 also apply to every workplace and require all risks to be assessed and controlled.

1 Managing health and safety

Not all risks may be easy to spot. Some may be obvious and quite likely to happen, such as slipping in a place where floors are often wet. Others may be less obvious, but could have such serious consequences that you need to make sure the risks are controlled, eg going onto a roof for cleaning or repairs.

Where to get help

In general, the bigger the risk, the more information and guidance you will need. This book may tell you much of what you need to know. Other sources of information and advice include:

- knowledge of good practice in the industry;
- guidance and advice from industry bodies and HSE;
- experience of accidents and 'near miss' injuries, or illness caused by work;
- the experience of employees.

It helps to know what the most common causes of injury, ill health and death at work are across all businesses in the UK – see the 'Introduction' section for more details.

Small businesses may find the web-based Health and Safety Performance Indicator helpful (www.businesslink.co.uk). This will help you assess how well you are managing your health and safety performance by taking you through most of the common risks and suggesting an action plan.

Competent advice

Although you can probably find out most of what you need to know for yourself, you might find that you are dealing with issues that need technical knowledge you have not got. In that case, you need to have a source of competent advice.

If not already available in-house, there are many people you can turn to for help – employers' organisations, trade associations, chambers of commerce, local training organisations, local health and safety groups, trade unions, insurance companies, suppliers of plant, equipment and chemicals, and consultants.

You can get information on specific issues by ringing HSE's Infoline (Tel: 0845 345 0055).

Keeping a record

If you employ five or more people you have to write down the main conclusions of your risk assessment. For most people this does not need to be a big exercise – just note the main points down about the significant risks and what you concluded, eg using short bullet points.

You should write down:

- the significant hazards, eg 'back injury when lifting packs of products';
- who is at risk, eg 'all workers in the storeroom';
- what more you need to do and why, eg 'explore bulk delivery or mechanical lifting to reduce the risk of back injury to workers lifting heavier packs'.

Remember, though, that the test of a good risk assessment is not how good your paperwork is, it is your practical understanding of the main risks in your work and what you need to do about them. If a risk is trivial and could not realistically result in any significant harm you do **not** need to write anything down.

Control the risks that need it

Pick out the priorities for action

The aim of risk assessment is to identify what more you need to do. If, like many businesses, you find that there are quite a lot of improvements that you could make, big and small, don't try to do everything at once. Make a plan of action to deal with the most important things first. A good plan to act on the findings of your risk assessment often includes a mixture of different things:

- a few cheap or easy improvements that can be done quickly, perhaps as a temporary solution until more reliable controls are in place;
- long-term solutions to risks which are the most likely to cause accidents or ill health, eg slips and trips or heavy lifting;
- long-term solutions to risks with the worst potential consequences, eg falls from height or an explosion;
- arrangements for training employees on the main risks that cannot be eliminated and how best to avoid them;
- clear responsibilities – who will lead on what, and by when;
- realistic dates for completing any improvements.

What do I have to do?

- Decide what could cause harm to people as a result of your business and what precautions you are going to take. This is your risk assessment.
- Decide how you will manage health and safety in your business. If you have five or more employees, you must write this down. This is your health and safety policy.
- Display a current certificate as required by the Employers' Liability (Compulsory Insurance) Act 1969, if you employ anyone.
- Provide free health and safety training for your employees so they know what hazards they may face and how to deal with them (see Chapter 21).
- You must have competent advice to help you meet your health and safety duties. This can involve employees from your business, external consultants or a combination of both.
- Provide toilets, washing facilities and drinking water for all your employees, including those with disabilities (see Chapters 2 and 23).
- Consult union safety representatives, representatives of employee safety or employees on health and safety matters (see Chapter 20).
- Display the Health and Safety Law poster for employees, or give out the leaflet with the same information.
- Notify certain work-related incidents, accidents and occupational diseases (see Chapter 25).
- Do not employ children under school leaving age in an industrial undertaking, except on authorised work experience schemes (see Chapter 23).
- Notify your local HSE office or Environmental Health Department if you start a new commercial or industrial business or relocate one (contact HSE's Infoline 0845 345 0055 for details).

Choosing solutions

There can be a number of ways to control the risks you identify as a priority for action. Do not make the mistake of only going for options that seem easy and cheap but may not work reliably, eg giving employees instructions that are difficult to follow.

If you are dealing with a relatively common risk, it is often easiest to identify a suitable solution from the guidance HSE publishes in print and on its website (www.hse.gov.uk) and put it into practice.

Solutions which may appear expensive can actually save you money if you combine them with improvements to your business, eg ordering bulk materials in big bags that can be lifted mechanically rather than hand-lifting lots of smaller bags, freeing your employees to do something else.

Starting with the best and most effective, the ways to deal with risks are:

- Get rid of the risk altogether. For example, avoid the need to work at heights by moving things to ground level, stop using highly flammable chemicals if you don't really need them, or change the layout of work so vehicles like lift trucks do not need to go through areas where there are pedestrians.
- Swap for a lower risk. For example reduce the weight of things that need lifting, or use pedestrian-operated pallet trucks instead of lift trucks.
- Separate the risks from people. For example put barriers between pedestrians and traffic, put guards on dangerous machinery, or use fixed pipes to pump dangerous liquids along rather than manual carrying and pouring.
- Give people rules, procedures, training or personal protective equipment. These rely on people always being careful and never making mistakes.

Make sure the risks stay controlled

Putting the right risk controls in place is important, but making sure they stay controlled is just as important.

- Make sure everyone is clear who has responsibility for what. All employers have to summarise this in a health and safety policy. If you employ five or more people you should write this policy down and show it to them. Employees also have responsibilities to co-operate with their employer's efforts to improve health and safety and to look out for each other.
- Make regular, planned checks of the workplace to look for risks that may have been overlooked, or people who are not working safely. Remember that things change – equipment wears out, people forget their training, and do not always follow rules, especially when they think they have found a quicker or better way of getting the job done.
- Do not forget maintenance. Be guided by manufacturers' recommendations when working out your own maintenance schedules for items such as vehicles, lift trucks, ventilation plant, ladders, portable

electrical equipment, protective clothing and equipment, and machine guards.

- Investigate when things go wrong. If there is an injury or near-miss, don't just blame someone or look for a quick fix. Use your investigation to learn more about how well you are managing health and safety.

- Follow up absences from work. There may be a work-related illness you did not know about, or there could be things that you can do to help people get back to work (see Chapter 19).

- Review where you are every year or two, to make sure you are still improving or at least not sliding back. Look at your health and safety policy and risk assessment again. Have there been any changes? Are there improvements you still need to make? Have you learnt something from accidents or near-misses? Make sure your risk assessments stay up to date.

Inspectors and the law

Health and safety laws which apply to your business are enforced by an inspector either from HSE or from your local authority. Their job is to see how well you are dealing with your workplace hazards, especially the more serious ones which could lead to injuries or ill health. They may wish to investigate an accident or a complaint. Inspectors do visit workplaces without notice but you are entitled to see their identification before letting them in.

Don't forget that they are there to give help and advice, particularly to smaller businesses who may not have a lot of knowledge. When they do find problems they will aim to deal with you in a reasonable and fair way. If you are not satisfied with the way you have been treated, take the matter up with the inspector's manager. Your complaint will be investigated, and you will be told what is to be done to put things right if a fault is found.

Inspectors have the right of entry to your premises, the right to talk to employees and safety representatives and to take photographs and samples. They are entitled to your co-operation and answers to questions.

If there is a problem they have the right to issue a notice requiring improvements to be made, or (where a risk of serious personal injury exists) one which stops a process or the use of dangerous equipment. If you receive an improvement or prohibition notice you have the right to appeal to an industrial tribunal.

Inspectors do have the power to prosecute a business or, under certain circumstances, an individual for breaking health and safety law, but they will take your attitude and safety record into account.

Find out more

Management of health and safety at work. Management of Health and Safety at Work Regulations 1999. Approved Code of Practice and guidance L21 (Second edition) ISBN 0 7176 2488 9

Successful health and safety management HSG65 (Second edition) ISBN 0 7176 1276 7

Health and safety law poster
Encapsulated ISBN 0 7176 2493 5
Rigid PVC ISBN 0 7176 1779 3

Employers' Liability (Compulsory Insurance) Act 1969: A guide for employers Leaflet HSE40(rev1)

Five steps to risk assessment Leaflet INDG163(rev1)

An introduction to health and safety: Health and safety in small businesses Leaflet INDG259(rev1)

Need help on health and safety? Guidance for employers on when and how to get advice on health and safety Leaflet INDG322

Reduce risks – cut costs: The real costs of accidents and ill health at work Leaflet INDG355

Visit the risk management pages on HSE's website at: www.hse.gov.uk/risk

2

The hazards

You must provide a safe and healthy environment for all your employees. You also need to take account of their welfare needs. You will need to consider, for example, lighting, ventilation, temperature, toilets and washing facilities.

Assess your own working environment by using the guidelines in this chapter.

Don't forget any people with disabilities who may need special toilet and washing facilities, wide doorways and gangways.

Also see Chapter 3 for information on slips and trips and Chapter 4 for information on fire safety.

The workplace

A safe place of work

You must:

- make sure your buildings are in good repair;
- maintain the workplace and any equipment so that it is safe and works efficiently;
- put right any dangerous defects immediately, or take steps to protect anyone at risk;
- take precautions to prevent people or materials falling from open edges, eg fencing or guard-rails;
- fence or cover floor openings, eg vehicle examination pits, when not in use;
- have enough space for safe movement and access, eg to machinery;
- provide safe glazing, if necessary (eg protected, toughened or thick) which is marked to make it easy to see;
- make sure floors, corridors and stairs etc are free of obstructions, eg trailing cables;
- provide good drainage in wet processes;
- have windows that can be opened and cleaned safely. They should be designed to stop people falling out or bumping into them when open. You may need to fit anchor points if window cleaners have to use harnesses;
- provide weather protection for outdoor workplaces, if practical;
- keep outdoor routes safe during icy conditions, eg salt/sand and sweep them.

Also think about:

- siting machinery and furniture so that sharp corners do not stick out;
- not overloading floors;
- providing space for storing tools and materials;
- marking the edges of openings like vehicle pits;
- finding out the views of employees on the design of the workplace.

The law

Look at the Workplace (Health, Safety and Welfare) Regulations 1992 for the full requirements.

The Health and Safety (Display Screen Equipment) Regulations 1992 (as amended) apply where staff habitually use computers and other display screens as a significant part of their normal work.

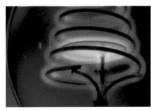

Lighting

You must provide:

- good light – use natural light where possible but try to avoid glare;
- a good level of local lighting at workstations where necessary;
- suitable forms of lighting. Some fluorescent tubes flicker and can be dangerous with some rotating machinery because the rotating part can appear to have stopped;
- special fittings for flammable or explosive atmospheres, eg from paint spraying;
- well-lit stairs and corridors.

Think about:

- having light-coloured walls to improve brightness (but darker colours to reduce arc-welding flash).

Moving around the premises

You must have:

- safe passage for pedestrians and vehicles – you may need separate routes (see Chapter 11);
- level, even surfaces without holes or broken boards (see Chapter 3);
- hand-rails on stairs and ramps where necessary;
- safe doors, eg vision panels in swing doors, sensitive edges on power doors;
- surfaces which are not slippery;
- well-lit outside areas – this will help security.

Think about:

- marking steps, kerbs and fixed obstacles, eg by black and yellow diagonal stripes.

HSE Infoline 0845 345 0055 HSE website www.hse.gov.uk HSE Books 01787 881165

Designing workstations

Make sure:

- workstations and seating fit the worker and the work;
- backrests support the small of the back and you must provide footrests if necessary;
- work surfaces are at a suitable height;
- there is easy access to controls on equipment.

Think about:

- providing well-designed tools to reduce hand or forearm injury from repeated awkward movements;
- reducing exposure to hazardous substances, noise, heat or cold, eg by using local exhaust ventilation or engineering controls – there is more about these in later chapters.

Display screen equipment (DSE)

What must employers do by law?

- Identify what display screen equipment and users in your workplace are covered.
- Assess workstations and meet the minimum requirements for them.
- Plan the work so there are breaks or changes of activity.
- On request provide eye and eyesight tests, and spectacles if special ones are necessary.
- Provide training and information.

What does this mean in practice?

Ensure that:

- risks are assessed and reduced;
- all workstations meet the minimum requirements for:
  - equipment such as screens and keyboards;
  - desks;
  - chairs;
  - the working environment; and
  - software;
- work is planned so that there are breaks or changes of activity;
- users are given training and information;
- eye tests are provided on request.

Find out more

Work with display screen equipment. Health and Safety (Display Screen Equipment) Regulations 1992 as amended by the Health and Safety (Miscellaneous Amendments) Regulations 2002. Guidance on Regulations L26 (Second edition) ISBN 0 7176 2582 6

The law on VDUs: An easy guide HSG90 ISBN 0 7176 2602 4

Working with VDUs Leaflet INDG36(rev2)

2 The workplace

Cleanliness

You must:

- provide clean floors and stairs, which are drained and not slippery (see Chapter 3);
- provide clean premises, furniture and fittings (eg lights);
- provide containers for waste materials;
- remove dirt, refuse and trade waste regularly;
- clear up spillages promptly;
- eliminate traps for dirt or germs, eg by sealing joints between surfaces;
- keep internal walls or ceilings clean. They may need painting to help easy cleaning.

Hygiene and welfare

You must provide:

- clean, well-ventilated toilets (separate for men and women unless each convenience has its own lockable door);
- wash basins with hot and cold (or warm) running water;
- showers for dirty work or emergencies;
- soap and towels (or a hand dryer);
- skin cleansers, with nail brushes where necessary;
- barrier cream and skin-conditioning cream where necessary;
- special hygiene precautions where necessary, eg where food is handled or prepared;
- drying facilities for wet clothes;
- certain facilities for workers working away from base, eg chemical toilets in some circumstances;
- lockers or hanging space for clothing;
- changing facilities where special clothing is worn;
- a clean drinking water supply (marked if necessary to distinguish it from the non-drinkable supply);
- rest facilities, including facilities for eating food which would otherwise become contaminated;
- arrangements to protect non-smokers from discomfort caused by tobacco smoke in any separate rest areas, eg provide separate areas or rooms for smokers and non-smoking or prohibit smoking in rest areas and rest rooms (see Chapter 19);
- rest facilities for pregnant women and nursing mothers (see Chapter 23).

Comfortable conditions

You must provide:

- a reasonable working temperature in workrooms – usually at least 16°C, or 13°C for strenuous work;
- local heating or cooling where a comfortable temperature cannot be maintained throughout each workroom (eg hot and cold processes);
- thermal clothing and rest facilities where necessary, eg for 'hot work' or cold stores;
- good ventilation – avoid draughts;
- heating systems which do not give off dangerous or offensive levels of fume into the workplace;
- enough space in workrooms.

Remember that noise can be a nuisance as well as damaging to health (see Chapter 13).

Find out more

Workplace health, safety and welfare. Workplace (Health, Safety and Welfare) Regulations 1992. Approved Code of Practice L24 ISBN 0 7176 0413 6

Thermal comfort in the workplace: Guidance for employers HSG194 ISBN 0 7176 2468 4

Lighting at work HSG38 (Second edition) ISBN 0 7176 1232 5

Seating at work HSG57 (Second edition) ISBN 0 7176 1231 7

Workplace health, safety and welfare: A short guide for managers Leaflet INDG244

Welfare at work: Guidance for employers on welfare provisions Leaflet INDG293

Slips and trips

The hazards

A third of major injuries in the workplace, such as broken bones, serious burns, and loss of consciousness, are caused by someone slipping or tripping.

Slips and trips also account for half of all the reported injuries to members of the public in workplaces where there is public access, such as shops, restaurants and hospitals.

Slips and trips often cause other types of accidents and in some situations the potential for serious injury is much greater. People working in kitchens who slip or trip are at risk of being scalded, people working on high platforms who slip or trip may fall from height, and slipping while carrying a load may cause a strained back.

The basic requirements for preventing slips and trips

- Floors must not have holes or slopes, or be uneven or slippery so that people might be put at risk.
- Floors in a workplace must be kept free from obstructions and from any article or substance that may cause a person to slip, trip or fall.

Slips: What to look for

- People rarely slip on clean, dry floors. If your floor gets contaminated with water, other liquids, dirt, dust or anything else then you may have a problem.
- If the floor has a smooth surface, eg vinyl, polished surfaces, ceramic tiles or metal, even a tiny amount of contamination can be a real slip problem. Floors with higher surface roughness generally have better slip resistance.

Work through each of the following points in turn to see what you can do about slip risks.

The law

Look at the Workplace (Health, Safety and Welfare) Regulations 1992 for full details.

Stop the floor getting wet or contaminated in the first place

- Maintain equipment to stop leaks.
- Clean floors to a dry finish.
- Control and contain processes to prevent spillages and splashes.

Stop contamination from getting onto the walkways

- Stop water getting walked in on people's feet, eg provide good entrance matting.
- Site 'messy' activities away from walkways.
- Extract ventilation can stop steam and grease being deposited on floors.

If floor contamination does happen, deal with it

- Clean up spillages immediately.
- If floors are left wet after cleaning, stop anyone walking on them until they are dry.
- Have procedures for both routine and 'spillage response' cleaning.

Get the best grip you can from your existing floor

- A floor gets its grip from its surface roughness. Poorly cleaned floors lose that roughness – and grip. Good cleaning maintains and can even restore surface grip.
- Check you are using the right cleaning methods and products for your floor.

HSE Infoline 0845 345 0055 **HSE website** www.hse.gov.uk **HSE Books** 01787 881165

Increase the grip of the existing floor

- Some floors can be treated (non-slip paint, etching etc) to provide more surface roughness and more grip.
- Stick-on anti-slip strips can be sometimes be useful (but be sure they don't cause a trip hazard).
- Anti-slip treatments might only work for a while. Keep a check on them over time.

Replace the floor surface with one with better grip

- If you have gone through the first five steps and still have a slip problem then a new floor surface is probably needed.
- Think about how your floor is used and what type of contaminant will get onto it and then specify a floor surface that has enough grip to deal with that.
- Make sure that you use the right cleaning system for your new floor or it might not last or may lose its grip.

Trips: What to look for

Floors in poor condition and bad housekeeping are responsible for most trip injuries at work. If you answer 'yes' to any of these questions you need to take action. These are common problems but there may be others.

- Trip injuries are often caused because floor surfaces have become damaged or uneven. Do yours need improvement or repair?
- Are cables or pipes sometimes allowed to trail where people walk?
- Many trip injuries are caused simply by things being left where they should not be. Are there any obstructions in your work areas or walkways?
- Can any mats slip about?
- Do mats or floor tiles curl up at the edges?
- Are there any changes in level such as slopes or a step that might not be plainly seen?
- Can deliveries sometimes clog up walkways and working areas?
- At busy times do you sometimes run out of space to put down goods and materials that you are working on or with?

13

What else can cause a slip or trip accident?

- Look out for poor lighting, shadows and glare, as people are more likely to be injured if it is difficult for them to see where they are going.
- Trip or slip hazards near distractions are especially dangerous, eg sudden loud noises or displays which deliberately divert people's attention.
- Are people rushing, carrying loads, pushing or pulling things?
- Might some pedestrians be less steady on their feet or more at risk such as visually impaired people, older people, mothers with young children?
- Are all pedestrians familiar with the layout and walkway routes?
- Have employees been instructed and trained in how to prevent slips and trips? Do they know what is expected of them?

What about footwear?

- Wearing suitable footwear can sometimes help prevent slips and trips.
- Footwear used to try to deal with slips and trips is classed as personal protective equipment (PPE). Do everything you can to deal with contamination and floor problems first and use PPE as a last resort (see Chapter 24).
- The right 'non-slip' footwear can help but won't work everywhere. Some types of footwear marked as 'anti-slip' might not provide any additional protection in some workplaces.
- If you can, carry out a trial of any footwear you choose to make sure it is suitable for your workplace and workforce. Always include employees in the choosing process or they might not wear it.
- Specialist footwear might not be necessary - adopting a 'sensible shoe' policy for all employees might be enough.

Find out more

Slips and trips: Guidance for employers on identifying hazards and controlling risks HSG155 ISBN 0 7176 1145 0

Preventing slips and trips at work Leaflet INDG225(rev1)

The assessment of pedestrian slip risk: The HSE approach www.hse.gov.uk/pubns/web/slips01.pdf (web only)

Slips and trips: The importance of floor cleaning www.hse.gov.uk/pubns/web/slips02.pdf (web only)

Visit HSE's slips and trips web pages: www.hse.gov.uk/slips

HSE Infoline 0845 345 0055 HSE website www.hse.gov.uk HSE Books 01787 881165

General fire safety

The hazards

General fire safety covers the steps that need to be taken to avoid fires in the workplace and the precautions required to protect people if there is a fire.

For fire to start, three things are needed: a source of ignition (heat), a source of fuel (something that burns) and oxygen.

Sources of ignition:
eg heaters, lighting, naked flames, electrical equipment, hot processes (such as welding or grinding), smokers' materials (cigarettes, matches etc), and anything else that can get very hot or cause sparks.

Sources of fuel:
eg flammable liquids (petrol, paint, varnish, white spirit etc), wood, paper, plastic, rubber or foam, liquefied petroleum gas (LPG), loose packaging materials, waste rubbish, furniture.

Sources of oxygen:
the air around us and also some chemicals (oxidising materials) and oxygen supplies from cylinders etc.

You must carry out a fire risk assessment

You must carry out a fire risk assessment and under current law (which will change on 1 October 2006) you must also decide whether your business requires you to obtain a fire certificate. For futher advice contact your local fire and rescue authority.

Your fire risk assessment can be done as part of the general risk assessment required under health and safety law (see Chapter 1). This will enable you to identify and then take steps to eliminate, reduce or control risks to prevent injury from fire.

Identify fire hazards

Identify any ignition sources and sources of fuel at your workplace (see 'The hazards').

Identify people at risk

If there is a fire, all people in and around the premises are at risk, however, some people may be at greater risk. This includes night staff or lone workers; people who are unfamiliar with the premises, such as visitors or customers; and children, the elderly and the disabled.

Evaluate the risks and take steps to reduce the risks and protect people

- Think about how a fire could start.
- Keep ignition sources and sources of fuel apart.
- Avoid accidental fire, eg do not put heaters where they could be knocked over.
- Fires can be caused deliberately, so do not leave potential sources of fuel around, eg check outside that rubbish is not lying around or allowed to build up.

The law

New fire safety legislation, the Regulatory Reform (Fire Safety) Order 2005, is due to come into force in England and Wales on 1 October 2006. In Scotland, Part 3 of the Fire (Scotland) Act 2005, which is concerned with fire safety and supported by the Fire Safety (Scotland) Regulations, is due to come into force in October 2006, at the earliest.

At most workplaces the local fire and rescue authority is responsible for enforcing general fire safety and if you need advice you should contact them.

4 General fire safety

Precautions to protect people if there is a fire

- How will a fire be detected, particularly in areas that are not frequently used?
- If a fire does start, how will people be warned, eg if you have a fire alarm, check regularly that it is working. Can it be heard everywhere over normal background noise?
- Is appropriate fire-fighting equipment available, eg enough fire extinguishers of the right type (and properly serviced) to deal promptly with small outbreaks?
- Will people be able to escape before the fire puts them at risk, eg are there enough clearly marked, unobstructed escape routes and fire doors that can be opened easily from the inside? Never wedge fire doors open.
- Do you have arrangements for anyone who needs help such as elderly or disabled people?
- Who will check that everyone gets out safely and who will call the local fire and rescue authority?
- How do you know that your fire precautions will work – do you check them regularly? Everyone should know what to do in case of fire – display clear instructions and have regular fire drills.

Record, plan and train

- Keep a record of the hazards you have identified and what you have done to remove or reduce them.
- Make a plan so you and your staff will know what to do if there is a fire. Take into account the findings of your risk assessment.
- Provide information, instruction and training to ensure people know what to do if there is a fire.
- Practise the fire drill.
- Is everyone with a role to play competent to carry out their role?
- If you share a building with others you should co-ordinate your plan with them.
- Where dangerous substances are stored or used in large enough quantities to make the risk more than slight, inform the local fire and rescue authority. (Also see Chapter 18 for information on flammable and explosive substances.)

Review the risk assessment

Review your risk assessment regularly and whenever you are planning to make significant changes to your premises or work practices, or if there is a fire or a 'near miss'.

What are the key features of the new fire legislation?

- In England and Wales, the Regulatory Reform (Fire Safety) Order 2005 is due to come into force on 1 October. In Scotland, Part 3 of the Fire (Scotland) Act 2005 is due to come into force in October 2006, at the earliest.
- Both will create a simplified fire-safety regime applying to most workplaces and other non-domestic premises.
- Both will be risk-assessment based with responsibility for fire safety in England and Wales resting with a 'responsible person', or equivalent person in Scotland with duties under Part 3 of the Fire (Scotland) Act 2005.
- There will be no separate certification system for higher risk premises (the Fire Certificate (Special Premises) Regulations will be removed and fire certificates will no longer be valid).
- Some self-employed people and parts of the voluntary sector, eg charity shops, will be included.

Find out more

A series of industry sector-specific guidance documents will be published to provide practical advice on how to comply with the new legislation. For more information, visit the websites for the Office of the Deputy Prime Minister (ODPM) (www.odpm.gov.uk) for England and Wales and the Scottish Executive (www.scotland.gov.uk) for Scotland.

The hazards

Falls from height result in around 60 deaths at work and about 4000 major injuries every year. One of the main causes is falls from ladders.

Also see Chapter 6 which deals with building work, roof work and scaffolds.

Work at height

What do I need to do?

You must ensure work at height is carried out safely. The Work at Height Regulations set out a hierarchy of control measures to follow when planning work at height.

Avoid work at height where you can

- Do as much work as possible from the ground or partly from the ground. For example, use long-handled poles when cleaning windows or use other equipment to avoid having to climb; assemble structures on the ground and lift them into position with lifting equipment.

Where you cannot avoid work at height

- Prevent falls. Use 'collective' prevention methods which include guard rails and working platforms (eg cradles, scaffolding, mobile elevating work platforms) before personal methods (eg a work restraint which stops the user getting into a position where they could fall).
- If you cannot eliminate the risk of a fall, take steps to minimise the distance and consequences of a fall, eg use nets or airbags. If you cannot use collective methods, use a fall-arrest lanyard, rope access and work-positioning techniques to protect against a fall.
- If you cannot minimise the distance and consequences of a fall, take other steps to ensure safe systems of work and to prevent the likelihood of a fall causing injury, eg instruction, information and training and ensuring the access equipment you use (such as ladders or kick stools) is well maintained and suitable for the work.

The law

The Work at Height Regulations came into force on 6 April 2005. They cover work in any place from which a person could fall far enough to cause personal injury.

The Regulations place duties on employers, the self-employed and others who have control over work at height. You must make sure that all work at height is properly planned, supervised and carried out by people who are competent to do the job.

Think about the following

- Make sure the surface/access equipment you use is stable and strong enough to support your weight and that of any equipment. Any edge protection should be wide enough and strong enough to prevent a fall.
- If you are working on or near a fragile surface, eg an asbestos cement roof, you must take precautions to prevent a fall or to minimise the distance and consequences of any fall if there is one.
- If you are working at height, make sure you can get safely to and from where you want to work and also consider emergency evacuation and rescue procedures.
- Make sure everyone involved is competent to do the work they are responsible for, including those who plan and organise the work.
- Consider the risks from working in extreme weather conditions – if the weather could endanger your health and safety, stop work until it is safe to continue.
- Choose the most appropriate equipment for the type of work being done and how often it will be used.
- Provide protection against falling objects.
- Make sure equipment used for work at height is well maintained and inspected regularly.

Ladders

Using ladders incorrectly causes about a quarter of falls which result in major injuries. Ladders should only be used where a risk assessment shows that the job is low risk and will not last long (up to a maximum of 15-30 minutes depending on the job) or where there are features of the site which mean that other equipment cannot be used.

- Ladders are often used when it would be better to use other equipment, eg mobile tower scaffolds, podium steps or mobile elevating work platforms (MEWPs).
- When choosing a ladder, you must make sure it is in good condition, eg no rungs are cracked or missing and the ladder feet are present and in good condition.
- Do a daily pre-use check (including the feet).
- Inspect the ladder periodically and make sure it is maintained properly.
- Do not use makeshift or homemade ladders or carry out makeshift repairs to a damaged ladder. Never paint ladders – this may hide defects.
- Position the ladder so that the bottom will not slip outwards. Use it at an angle of 75° (1 unit out for every 4 units up – the 1 in 4 rule).

- Secure ladders to prevent movement.
- Rest the top of the ladder against a solid surface.
- When placing the ladder, rest its foot on a firm, level surface and make sure the rungs are level. Do not place it on material or equipment to gain extra height.
- Make sure floor surfaces are clean and not slippery.
- Access ladders must extend at least 1 m above the landing places unless there is a suitable handhold to provide equivalent support.
- Extending ladders need an overlap of at least three rungs.

Using a ladder

- Always grip the ladder when climbing.
- Do not work off the top three rungs – these are to provide a handhold.
- Do not carry heavy items or long lengths of material up a ladder – use it for light work only.
- Carry light tools in a shoulder bag or holster attached to a belt so that you have both hands free to hold the ladder.
- Do not overreach.

Step ladders

- Do a daily pre-use check (including the feet).
- Inspect the step ladder periodically and make sure it is maintained properly.
- When in use make sure the rungs are level and it is resting on firm, level ground.
- Make sure floor surfaces are clean and not slippery.
- Make sure step ladders are used for light work only.
- Have enough space to fully open and use any locking devices provided.
- Do not work off the top two steps unless you have a safe handhold on the steps.
- Avoid side-on working.
- Do not overreach.

Find out more

The Work at Height Regulations 2005: A brief guide
Leaflet INDG401

Safe use of ladders and stepladders:
An employers' guide Leaflet INDG402

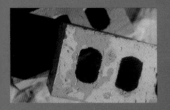

Building work

The hazards

Falling from height is the major cause of serious accidents when building or doing maintenance work on existing buildings (see Chapter 5 for the hierarchy of controls to follow for working at height and for detailed advice on using ladders and step ladders).

Other hazards include being struck by falling materials; striking buried electric cables or gas pipes; burial by excavation collapses; contact with electricity (see Chapter 15); exposure to harmful substances such as asbestos, paints, glues, or cleaning materials (see Chapter 17); and being run over by construction vehicles which can have poor driver visibility (see Chapter 11).

Construction work

Most activities involving building work are subject to the various Construction Regulations which specify standards for a wide range of issues such as safe access and safe lifting. The Regulations apply to construction, structural alteration, repair, maintenance, repointing, redecorating and external cleaning, demolition, site preparation and laying of foundations.

- If you are a contractor and building works are expected to last longer than 30 days or involve more than 500 days to complete the work you must notify your HSE inspector.
- If you use a contractor you still have legal responsibility for many matters on your premises (see Chapter 22).

Before you start

- Can you do the work in a different way to make it safer?
- Plan the work to remove or reduce the risks.
- Don't take on work for which you are unprepared.
- You may need specialist help with, eg demolition of buildings, digging deep trenches or roofing.

The law

Look at the Workplace (Health, Safety and Welfare) Regulations 1992, the Provision and Use of Work Equipment Regulations 1998 (PUWER) and the Work at Height Regulations 2005.

If you are a builder, look at the Construction (Health, Safety and Welfare) Regulations 1996, which apply instead of the Workplace Regulations.

The Construction (Design and Management) Regulations 1994 place additional duties on principal contractors, clients, designers and planning supervisors.

6 Building work

Protect other people

- Use barriers or fences to keep people out of the workplace.
- Use signs to warn people of specific dangers.
- Do not allow material to be dropped where it will cause a risk of injury.
- Keep children away from all building work.

Using a contractor for building work

- Clearly identify all aspects of the work you want the contractor to do and consider the associated health and safety implications.
- Provide information to the contractor on any site- or task-specific hazards, eg if a surface is fragile.
- Choose a contractor who you are satisfied is competent to do the work without putting themselves or other people at risk.
- Obtain a method statement written by the contractor specifying the precautions required to carry out the work safely.
- Monitor their work to make sure the job is being done safely as agreed.
- When the work is finished check that the area is left in a safe condition.

Mobile tower scaffolds

Erecting the tower

- Be trained in the safe erection and use of tower scaffolds. Follow the manufacturer's instructions – do not exceed the maximum height allowed for a given base dimension. Lock any wheels and extend outriggers.
- Do not mix components from different types of scaffold or use damaged components.
- It must rest on firm, level ground – securely lock any wheels before use.
- Provide a safe way to get to and from the work platform, eg by an internal ladder. It is not safe to climb up the outside.
- Working platforms must be provided with guard rails and toe boards.
- Tie the tower rigidly to the structure if it is likely to be exposed to strong winds, or if materials are lifted up the outside of the tower.
- You must not overload the working platform. Do not apply pressure, which could overturn the tower.
- Do not cover the tower with sheeting.
- Never work off a ladder placed on top of the working platform.

Moving the tower

- Check there are no power lines in the way or obstructions, holes etc in the ground.
- Do not allow people or materials to remain on the tower.
- Beware of towers 'running away with you' when being moved down or across slopes.

HSE Infoline 0845 345 0055 **HSE website** www.hse.gov.uk **HSE Books** 01787 881165

General access scaffolds

When providing a scaffold you must make sure:

- it is erected, altered or dismantled by competent scaffolders;
- scaffolding in public areas does not endanger people passing nearby while it is being erected or used;
- the scaffolders understand what you want to use the scaffold for. Never add sheeting to a scaffold without telling the scaffolders;
- you know how much load the scaffold can carry. Never overload a scaffold;
- it is properly tied – never alter a scaffold or remove ties, boards, and handrails. Such work should be done by a trained scaffolder;
- working platforms have guard rails and toe boards. Brick guards or similar will often be needed to provide extra protection to prevent materials falling;
- platforms are wide enough for the work to be done, boards are properly supported and do not overhang too much (at least three supports not more than 1.5 m apart);
- stairs or a ladder tower are provided for safe access between each level or lift;
- the scaffold is inspected at least once a week, or whenever it is substantially altered or after very bad weather;
- the person doing the inspection fully understands scaffold safety and records the results.

If you are going to work on a scaffold someone has provided for you, don't start work without checking the above points (including a look at the inspection register).

Roof work

When working on a roof you must:

- always establish if the roof is or has become fragile or contains fragile material. Falls through fragile materials are a major cause of fatal accidents;
- have safe access onto and off the roof, eg by a general access or tower scaffold;
- use edge protection at the open edge/eaves level of a roof to stop people and materials falling off it;
- cover openings and fragile materials such as roof lights or provide barriers around them;
- have safe means of moving across the roof. On sloping roofs you will need purpose-made roof ladders. Do not use homemade ladders or boards as these have caused many accidents;
- not walk along the line of the roof bolts above the purlins or along the roof edge of a fragile roof – this is as unsafe as walking a tightrope;
- place prominent warning notices where someone can approach a fragile surface;
- have safe means of getting material up onto the roof;
- never throw materials, old slates, tiles etc from the roof or scaffold where this could cause injury. Use enclosed debris chutes or lower the debris in skips or baskets.

You should:

- Provide permanent means of safe access, eg to plant rooms, ventilation equipment, and roof lights that need cleaning.

HSE Infoline 0845 345 0055 HSE website www.hse.gov.uk HSE Books 01787 881165

Ground work

- Identify the location of underground services before starting to dig.
- Dig well away from underground services such as electricity cables, gas pipes etc. If you have to work near services, use service plans, locators and safe digging practices to avoid danger.
- Trench and excavation sides can collapse suddenly whatever the nature of the soil. Always assess whether an excavation needs to have the sides sloped back or supported.

Other hazards

- Paints, glues, cleaning materials etc used during maintenance may be a health risk – use the information from manufacturers and suppliers to identify hazards (see Chapter 17).
- Beware of gases found in sewers, and fumes or lack of oxygen in confined spaces (see Chapter 8).

Find out more

Health and safety in roof work HSG33 (Second edition) ISBN 0 7176 1425 5

Avoiding danger from underground services HSG47 (Second edition) ISBN 0 7176 1744 0

Health and safety in construction HSG150 (Second edition) ISBN 0 7176 2106 5

Managing health and safety in construction: Construction (Design and Management) Regulations 1994. Approved Code of Practice and guidance HSG224 ISBN 0 7176 2139 1

A guide to the Construction (Health, Safety and Welfare) Regulations 1996 Leaflet INDG220

Machinery safety

The hazards

Moving machinery can cause injury in many ways.

Hair or clothing can become entangled and drag a person into rotating parts, and parts of the body can be drawn in or trapped between rollers, belts and pulley drives.

People can be crushed, both between parts moving together or towards a fixed part of the machine, wall or other object, and two parts moving past one another can cause shearing.

People can be struck and injured by moving parts of machinery or ejected material.

Sharp edges can cause cuts and severing injuries, sharp pointed parts can cause stabbing or puncture the skin, and rough surface parts can cause friction or abrasion.

Parts of the machine, materials and emissions (such as steam or water) can be hot or cold enough to cause burns or scalds and electricity can cause accidents (see Chapter 15).

Assess the risks

Before you start:

- check, before using any machine, that it is complete and free from defects;
- look at the residual risks identified by the manufacturer in their information/instructions provided with the machine and deal with them;
- put procedures in place for using and maintaining the machine;
- take care to ensure every static machine is stable (usually fixed down);
- choose the right machine for the job and do not site machines where customers or visitors may go and be exposed to risk.

Make sure the machine is safe:

- for any work which has to be done in setting up, maintenance, repair, breakdowns and removing blockages, as well as normal use;
- to be used, not only by experienced and well-trained workers, but also by new starters, people who have changed jobs or those who have particular difficulties;
- to be used by workers who may act foolishly or carelessly or make mistakes.

Make sure you deal with the risks from:

- electrical, hydraulic or pneumatic power supplies;
- badly designed safeguards being inconvenient to use or easily defeated, which could encourage your workers to risk injury and break the law.

What suppliers must do

- By law the supplier must provide the right safeguards and inform buyers of any risks ('residual risks') that users need to deal with because they could not be designed out.

The law

The Provision and Use of Work Equipment Regulations 1998 (PUWER) contain the requirements for work equipment to be safe.

Manufacturers and suppliers have duties to provide safe equipment. If in doubt, ask your inspector.

Guards

- You must use fixed guards (eg secured with screws or nuts and bolts) to enclose the dangerous parts, whenever practical.
- Think about the best materials to use – plastic may be easy to see through but can easily be damaged. Where you use wire mesh or similar materials, make sure the holes are not large enough to allow access to moving parts.
- If you have to go near dangerous parts regularly and fixed guards are not practical, you must use other methods, eg interlock the guard so that the machine cannot start before the guard is closed and cannot be opened while the machine is still moving.
- In some cases, eg guillotines, trip systems such as photo-electric devices, pressure-sensitive mats or automatic guards may be used if fixed or interlocked guards are not practical.
- Some machines are controlled by programmable electronic systems. Your supplier must tell you about the safety of the system. Changes to routine working or main programmes should only be carried out by a competent person. Keep a record of programming changes and check they have been done properly.
- Where guards cannot give full protection, use jigs, holders, push sticks etc if practical.
- Make sure the guards you use allow the machine to be cleaned safely.

Machine operation

- Some workers, eg if they are young, inexperienced or have a disability, may be particularly at risk and will need extra instruction, training or supervision.
- Sometimes formal qualifications are needed, eg for chainsaw operators.
- You must never allow children to operate or to help at machines.
- All machine operators must be trained and, if necessary, given protective clothing (see Chapters 21 and 24).
- You must provide adequate lighting for all machines.

Machinery maintenance

■ You must make sure the guards and other safety devices are checked and kept in working order.
■ If maintenance workers need to remove guards or other safety devices, make sure the machine is stopped first or is safe and cannot be restarted, eg by having a lock-off system (see Chapter 20).
■ Make sure no one is defeating or getting around the guards or safety devices and, if they are, make sure it does not happen again.
■ Check the safeguarding after any modifications.
■ When putting in new machines, think about safe maintenance.

Machine controls

You must:

■ ensure control switches are clearly marked to show what they do;
■ have emergency stop controls where necessary, eg mushroom-head push buttons within easy reach;
■ make sure operating controls are designed and placed to avoid accidental operation, eg by shrouding start buttons and pedals.

7 Machinery safety

Operator's checklist

Check every time that:

- you know how to stop the machine before you start it;
- all guards are in position and all protective devices are working;
- the area around the machine is clean, tidy and free from obstructions;
- you tell your supervisor at once if you think a machine is not working properly or any safeguards are faulty;
- you are wearing appropriate protective clothing and equipment, such as safety glasses or shoes (see Chapter 24).

Never:

- use a machine unless you are authorised and trained to do so;
- try to clean a machine in motion – switch it off and unplug it or lock it off;
- use a machine or appliance which has a danger sign or tag attached to it. Danger signs should be removed only by an authorised person who is satisfied that the machine or process is now safe;
- wear dangling chains, loose clothing, gloves, rings or have long hair which could get caught up in moving parts;
- distract people who are using machines.

Find out more

Safe use of work equipment. Provision and Use of Work Equipment Regulations 1998. Approved Code of Practice and guidance L22 (Second edition) ISBN 0 7176 1626 6

Safe use of power presses. Provision and Use of Work Equipment Regulations 1998 as applied to power presses. Approved Code of Practice and guidance L112 ISBN 0 7176 1627 4

Safe use of lifting equipment. Lifting Operations and Lifting Equipment Regulations 1998. Approved Code of Practice and guidance L113 ISBN 0 7176 1628 2

Safe use of woodworking machinery. Provision and Use of Work Equipment Regulations 1998 as applied to woodworking machinery. Approved Code of Practice and guidance L114 ISBN 0 7176 1630 4

Safety in the use of abrasive wheels HSG17 (Third edition) ISBN 0 7176 1739 4

Simple guide to the Provision and Use of Work Equipment Regulations 1998 Leaflet INDG291

HSE Infoline 0845 345 0055 **HSE website** www.hse.gov.uk **HSE Books** 01787 881165

Plant and equipment maintenance

The hazards

Maintenance is carried out to prevent problems arising and to put faults right. It may be part of a planned programme or may have to be carried out at short notice after a breakdown. It always involves non-routine activities.

Hazards can occur when machinery starts up accidentally or too early; when using hand tools and electrical equipment; during contact with materials which are normally enclosed in plant and equipment; and when entering vessels or confined spaces where there may be toxic materials or a lack of air.

Lack of communication or confusion can cause accidents where maintenance is carried out during normal production work or where different contractors are working together at the same time on a site.

Take extra care when getting up to and working at heights, or when doing work which requires access to unusual parts of the building (see Chapter 5).

Before you start

- Is the job necessary?
- Can it be done less often without increasing other risks?
- Should it be done by specialist contractors? Never take on work for which you are not prepared or not competent.
- Plan the work to cut down the risks, eg the difficulties in co-ordinating maintenance and routine work can be avoided if maintenance work is performed before start-up or at shut-down periods. Access is easier if equipment is designed with maintenance in mind.

Safe working areas

- You must provide safe access and a safe place of work (see Chapters 5 and 6 on using ladders and scaffolds).
- Ensure the safety of maintenance workers and others who may be affected, eg other employees or contractors.
- Set up signs and barriers and position people at key points if they are needed to control the risk.

The law

Look at the Provision and Use of Work Equipment Regulations 1998 (PUWER) and the Workplace (Health, Safety and Welfare) Regulations 1992 for the full requirements.

You may also need to consider the Confined Spaces Regulations 1997.

27

8 Plant and equipment maintenance

Safe plant

Plant and equipment must be made safe before maintenance starts.

You will normally need to:

- isolate electrical and other power supplies. Most maintenance should be carried out with the power off. If the work is near uninsulated overhead electrical conductors, eg close to overhead travelling cranes, cut the power off first;
- lock off machines if there is a chance the power could be switched back on;
- isolate plant and pipelines containing pressured fluid, gas, steam or hazardous material. Lock off isolating valves;
- support parts of plant which could fall;

- ensure moving plant is stopped;
- allow components which operate at high temperatures time to cool;
- place mobile plant in neutral gear, apply the brake and chock the wheels;
- safely clean out vessels containing flammable solids, liquids, gases or dusts and check them before hot work is carried out to prevent explosions. You may need specialist help and advice to do this safely. Avoid entering tanks and vessels where possible as this carries a very high risk. If required, get specialist help to ensure adequate precautions are taken (see 'Confined spaces');
- clean and check vessels containing toxic materials before work starts.

Confined spaces

A number of people are killed and seriously injured in the UK each year while working in confined spaces. Asphyxiation and toxic fumes are the two most common causes of death, but others include drowning in free-flowing solids, eg grain silos, and fire and explosions. Two or more people are often involved in these incidents. One person is overwhelmed and then others attempt to rescue them without being adequately prepared.

What is a confined space?

Some confined spaces are fairly easy to identify, eg closed tanks, vessels and sewers. Others are less obvious but may be equally dangerous, eg open-topped tanks and vats, closed and unventilated rooms and silos. Confined spaces exist in all sectors of industry, so it is not possible to provide a complete list. You should identify where these hazards arise in your workplace and take precautions.

Deal with confined spaces

- Identify all confined spaces.
- Do the work from outside where possible.
- If entry is necessary follow the guidelines in Chapter 20.

Appropriate precautions

- Isolate the vessel to stop dust, fume or hazardous substances getting in.

- Clean up to ensure fumes do not develop from residues etc while the work is being done.
- Test the atmosphere to check that it is free from toxic or flammable vapours and that there is enough fresh air.
- Make sure there is enough ventilation to ensure an adequate supply of fresh air.
- Use non-sparking tools.
- Do not use petrol or diesel equipment inside the confined space.
- Make sure rescue equipment and enough trained personnel are ready at hand for rescue and resuscitation.
- Use safe lighting (eg low voltage).

See Chapter 24 for protective clothing and equipment and Chapter 21 for selection and training.

Find out more

Safe work in confined spaces. Confined Spaces Regulations 1997. Approved Code of Practice, Regulations and guidance L101 ISBN 0 7176 1405 0

Safe work in confined spaces Leaflet INDG258

HSE Infoline 0845 345 0055 **HSE website** www.hse.gov.uk **HSE Books** 01787 881165

Clear working procedures

■ Use the manufacturer's maintenance instructions where provided.

■ Chapter 20 gives more information on safe systems, including the use of 'permits to work'.

Personal protective equipment

■ Maintenance staff must be given clothing and equipment which is appropriate for the job to be done (see Chapter 24).

Hand tools

You must ensure hand tools are properly maintained, eg:

■ **Hammers** – avoid split, broken or loose shafts and worn or chipped heads. Make sure heads are properly secured to the shafts.

■ **Files** – should have a proper handle. Never use them as levers.

■ **Chisels** – the cutting edge should be sharpened to the correct angle. Do not allow the head to spread to a mushroom shape – grind off the sides regularly.

■ **Screwdrivers** – should never be used as chisels, and hammers should never be used on them. Split handles are dangerous.

■ **Spanners** – avoid splayed jaws. Scrap any which show signs of slipping. Have enough spanners of the right size. Do not improvise by using pipes etc as extension handles.

Find out more

Safe use of work equipment. Provision and Use of Work Equipment Regulations 1998. Approved Code of Practice and guidance L22 (Second edition) ISBN 0 7176 1626 6

Workplace health, safety and welfare. Workplace (Health, Safety and Welfare) Regulations 1992. Approved Code of Practice L24 ISBN 0 7176 0413 6

Using work equipment safely Leaflet INDG229(rev1)

Simple guide to the Provision and Use of Work Equipment Regulations 1998 Leaflet INDG291

HSE Infoline 0845 345 0055 **HSE website** www.hse.gov.uk **HSE Books** 01787 881165

Vehicle repair

- Make sure brakes are applied and wheels are chocked. Always start and run engines with the brakes on and in neutral gear.
- Support vehicles on both jacks and axle stands (never rely on jacks alone).
- Always prop raised bodies.
- Beware of the explosion risk when draining and repairing fuel tanks, and from battery gases – do not drain petrol tanks over a pit.
- Take care not to short-circuit batteries.
- Use a tyre cage when inflating commercial tyres, particularly those with split rim wheels – explosions do happen!
- Avoid breathing asbestos dust from brake and clutch lining pads – the best approach is to use asbestos-free linings.
- Wear protective clothing when handling battery acid.
- Be aware of the risk from mineral oil contamination on hands and other parts of the body, eg for those changing engine oils. Good hygiene is essential including making sure overalls are cleaned regularly and that you wash your hands hands before going to the toilet to avoid transferring oil.

See Chapter 24 for more information on protective clothing and equipment.

Find out more

Health and safety in tyre and exhaust fitting premises HSG62 ISBN 0 7176 1686 X

Health and safety in motor vehicle repair HSG67 ISBN 0 7176 0483 7

Gas- and oil-fired equipment

The hazards

There is a danger of fire and explosion and of toxic fumes (carbon monoxide) from piped gas supplies and appliances if they are not properly installed and maintained.

Explosions can occur in gas- and oil-fired plant such as ovens, stoves and boilers.

Gas supply

- If you suspect a leak, turn off the supply and immediately call the Gas Emergency Freephone number 0800 111 999 for natural gas, or, for liquefied petroleum gas (LPG), your gas supplier.
- If in doubt, evacuate the building and inform the police as well as the emergency call centre or gas supplier.
- Do not check for leaks with a naked flame.
- Do not turn the gas back on until the leak has been dealt with by a competent person.

Appliances

You must:

- use a competent fitter to install, maintain or repair your appliances;
- not use any appliance you know or suspect is unsafe;
- check also that the room has adequate ventilation – do not block air inlets to prevent draughts, and do not obstruct flues and chimneys;
- get your appliances regularly serviced by a competent person.

Any business (including a self-employed person) which works on gas fittings in premises covered by the Gas Safety (Installation and Use) Regulations 1998, such as catering establishments, schools and hospitals but excluding factories, must be registered with the Council for Registered Gas Installers (CORGI).

It is important to check this by asking to see a CORGI identity card or checking with CORGI (Tel: 0870 401 2300). The reverse of the card details what kind of work the installer is able to do (see example of card overleaf).

The law

The Gas Safety (Installation and Use) Regulations 1998 cover gas appliances, both natural gas and LPG, in most premises except in factories, where the Health and Safety at Work etc Act 1974 (the HSW Act) requires an equivalent or higher standard to be met.

HSE Infoline 0845 345 0055 **HSE website** www.hse.gov.uk **HSE Books** 01787 881165

9 Gas- and oil-fired equipment

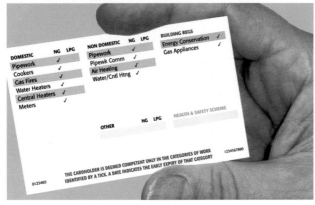

Plant

Explosions can be caused by ignition of unburnt fuel or flammable vapours from plant such as drying ovens on a paint-spraying line. There is a similar risk with electrically-heated equipment.

- Fit explosion relief and flame-failure protection as necessary.
- Interlock the heat source and the ventilation system if flammable vapours could build up to dangerous levels if there is a ventilation failure.
- Plant, including petrol-driven compressors and LPG-fuelled equipment, such as heaters and paint strippers, should be designed and operated to ensure there is enough air to burn the fuel properly.
- There should be enough ventilation to remove combustion products and solvents given off.
- Make sure the operators are fully trained – use a safe procedure for purging, lighting up and shutting down the plant.

Find out more

Safety in the installation and use of gas systems and appliances. Gas Safety (Installation and Use) Regulations 1998. Approved Code of Practice and guidance L56 (Second edition) ISBN 0 7176 1635 5

Gas appliances: Get them checked – keep them safe Leaflet INDG238(rev2)

Oil Firing Technical Association (OFTEC) Tel: 0845 65 85 080

HSE Gas safety advice line Tel: 0800 300 363

Pressurised plant and equipment

The hazards

If a piece of pressurised plant fails and bursts violently apart, the results can be devastating.

Many kinds of pressurised plant and equipment can produce a hazard, including steam boilers and associated pipework; pressurised hot water boilers and heating systems; air compressors, air receivers and associated pipework; autoclaves; chemical reaction vessels; slurry tankers; and high-pressure water jetting.

There will be further risks if the system contains harmful substances such as flammable or toxic materials.

There may be special risks associated with the maintenance of such plant (see Chapter 8).

Before you start

- Can the job be done another way without using pressurised equipment?
- Don't use high pressure when low pressure will do.

Good design and maintenance

- All plant and systems must be designed, constructed and installed to prevent danger and must have safety devices, such as pressure-relief valves.
- Systems must be properly maintained.
- Any modifications or repairs must be planned and not cause danger.
- There must be a written scheme for examination of pressure vessels, fittings and pipework, drawn up by a competent person.
- The examinations must be carried out.
- Records must be kept.

Safe operation

You must:

- operate plant within the safe operating limits. Sometimes these are laid down by the manufacturer or supplier. If not, a competent person can advise you, eg your Employers' Liability insurer;
- provide adequate instructions. This should include the manufacturer's operating manual which should have been provided in English by the supplier;
- provide instructions on what to do in an emergency.

The law

Look at the Pressure Systems Safety Regulations 2000 which deal with the safe operation of a pressure system and the Pressure Equipment Regulations 1999 which deal with the design, manufacture and supply of pressure systems.

HSE Infoline 0845 345 0055   HSE website www.hse.gov.uk   HSE Books 01787 881165

10 Pressurised plant and equipment

Pressure cleaning

- Follow the supplier's advice on high-pressure jetting equipment – protective clothing and keeping other people away are important, as is electrical safety.
- Avoid using compressed air for cleaning – instead use vacuum or low-pressure nozzles.
- Horseplay with compressed air is very dangerous and can be fatal.

Find out more

Safety of pressure systems. Pressure Systems Safety Regulations 2000. Approved Code of Practice L122 ISBN 0 7176 1767 X

Written schemes of examination: Pressure Systems Safety Regulations 2000 Leaflet INDG178(rev1)

Pressure systems: Safety and you Leaflet INDG261(rev1)

Workplace transport

The hazards

Every year over 5000 accidents involving transport in the workplace are reported. About 70 of these result in death.

People are knocked over, run over, or crushed against fixed parts by powered vehicles (eg LGVs, lift trucks and tractors) or by vehicles, plant and trailers which roll away when incorrectly parked.

People also fall from vehicles – either getting on or off, working at height, or when loading or unloading.

Moving materials mechanically is also hazardous and people can be crushed or struck by material when it falls from a lifting or moving device, or is dislodged from a storage stack.

Before you start

Think about whether there is an easier, safer way of doing the job.

You must carry out risk assessments for **all** transport activities, including loading and unloading. It can help if you:

- look carefully at all the vehicles and people moving round your worksite;
- mark the traffic and pedestrian movements on a plan of the site, so you can see the dangers clearly;
- identify areas where improvements are needed;
- remember to include less frequent tasks, eg waste skip changes;
- make sure you consider delivery drivers as they are particularly vulnerable.

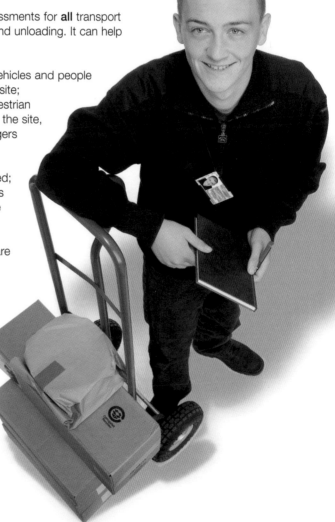

The law

Look at the Workplace (Health, Safety and Welfare) Regulations 1992 and the Provision and Use of Work Equipment Regulations 1998.

Look at the Lifting Operations and Lifting Equipment Regulations 1998 (LOLER) for the safe use of lifting equipment.

HSE Infoline 0845 345 0055 **HSE website** www.hse.gov.uk **HSE Books** 01787 881165

11 Workplace transport

Safe site

- Plan your workplace so that pedestrians are safe from vehicles.
- Provide separate routes for pedestrians and vehicles where possible.
- Where pedestrians and traffic meet, provide appropriate crossing points.
- Avoid reversing where possible.
- Provide a one-way system if you can.
- Use 'Highway code' signs to indicate vehicle routes, speed limits, pedestrian crossings etc.
- Make sure lighting is adequate where people and vehicles are working.
- Make sure road surfaces are firm and even.
- Make sure there are safe areas for loading and unloading.
- Visitors may not know your site, so try to provide separate car parking for them.

Safe driver

- Lift truck drivers must be trained as detailed in HSE's Approved Code of Practice L117 (see 'Find out more').
- Lift truck drivers need to be re-assessed at regular intervals, eg every three years, or when new risks arise such as changes to working practices.
- Drivers of other vehicles should be trained to a similar standard.
- Managers should actively supervise all drivers (including those visiting the site).

Safe vehicle

- Vehicles must be suitable for the purpose for which they are used.
- Vehicles must be maintained in good repair, particularly the braking system, steering, tyres, mirrors and specific safety systems.
- Remove the need for people to go up on vehicles where possible, eg by providing gauges and controls that are accessible from ground level.
- Reduce the risk of falling when people have to climb onto a vehicle or trailer by providing well-constructed ladders, non-slip walkways and guard rails where possible.
- Provide reversing aids such as CCTV (closed-circuit television) as appropriate.
- Fit roll-over protective structures and use seat belts where necessary.

HSE Infoline 0845 345 0055 **HSE website** www.hse.gov.uk **HSE Books** 01787 881165

Safe lifting by machine

Safe lifting needs to be planned. Any equipment you use must have been properly designed, manufactured and tested.

Consider:

- What are you are lifting?
- How heavy is it?
- Where is its centre of gravity?
- How will you attach it to the lifting machinery?
- Who is in control of the lift?
- What are the safe limits of the equipment?
- Could you rehearse the lift if necessary?

Also:

- Use only certified lifting equipment, marked with its safe working load, which is not overdue for examination.
- Keep the annual or six-monthly reports of thorough examination as well as any declarations of conformity or test certificates.
- Never use unsuitable equipment, eg makeshift, damaged, badly worn chains shortened with knots, kinked or twisted wire ropes, frayed or rotted fibre ropes.

- Never exceed the safe working load of machinery or accessories like chains, slings and grabs. Remember that the load in the legs of a sling increases as the angle between the legs increases.
- Do not lift a load if you doubt its weight or the adequacy of the equipment.
- Make sure the load is properly attached to the lifting equipment. If necessary, securely bind the load to prevent it slipping or falling off.
- Before lifting an unbalanced load, find out its centre of gravity. Raise it a few inches off the ground and pause – there will be little harm if it drops.
- Use packaging to prevent sharp edges of the load from damaging slings and do not allow tackle to be damaged by being dropped, dragged from under loads or subjected to sudden loads.
- When using jib cranes, make sure any indicators for safe loads are working properly and set correctly for the job and the way the machine is configured.
- Use outriggers where necessary.
- When using multi-slings make sure the sling angle is taken into account.
- Have a responsible slinger or banksman and use a recognised signalling system.
- Don't forget maintenance (see Chapter 8).

11 Workplace transport

Safe stacking

Materials and objects should be stored and stacked so they are not likely to fall and cause injury.

Do:

- stack on a firm, level base. Use a properly constructed rack when needed and secure it to the floor or wall if possible;
- use the correct container, pallet or rack for the job. Inspect these regularly for damage and reject defective ones;
- ensure stacks are stable, eg 'key' stacked packages of a uniform size like a brick wall so that no tier is independent of another;
- chock pipes and drums to prevent rolling and keep heavy articles near floor level.

Do not:

- exceed the safe load of racks, shelves or floors;
- allow items to stick out from stacks or bins into gangways;
- climb racks to reach upper shelves – use steps;
- lean heavy stacks against walls;
- de-stack by throwing down from the top or pulling out from the bottom.

Find out more

Workplace health, safety and welfare. Workplace (Health, Safety and Welfare) Regulations 1992. Approved Code of Practice L24 ISBN 0 7176 0413 6

Safe use of lifting equipment. Lifting Operations and Lifting Equipment Regulations 1998. Approved Code of Practice and guidance L113 ISBN 0 7176 1628 2

Rider-operated lift trucks. Operator training. Approved Code of Practice and guidance L117 ISBN 0 7176 2455 2

Safety in working with lift trucks HSG6 (Third edition) ISBN 0 7176 1781 5

Workplace transport safety: An employers' guide HSG136 (Second edition) ISBN 0 7176 6154 7

Workplace transport safety: An overview Leaflet INDG199(rev1)

Workplace transport site inspection checklist: https://www.hse.gov.uk/forms/transport/wtchk1.pdf

'Delivering safely' website: www.hse.gov.uk/workplacetransport/information/cooperation.htm

HSE Infoline 0845 345 0055 **HSE website** www.hse.gov.uk **HSE Books** 01787 881165

12

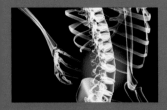

Lifting and handling

The hazards

Over a million people a year suffer from work-related back pain, repetitive strain injury (RSI) and similar problems affecting muscles, joints, and tendons.

Severe cases can badly affect both the employer and the injured person. Employers may have to bear large costs, eg for retraining, wages, overtime and civil liability. The injured person may find that their lifestyle, leisure activities, ability to sleep and job prospects are made worse.

There are many cost-effective ways to prevent or minimise such problems. You cannot prevent all injuries, so make sure there are systems in place for early reporting of symptoms, proper treatment and a managed return to work.

See Chapter 2 for information on how to reduce the risks from display screen equipment.

Are aches and pains a problem in my workplace?

If your work includes any of the following, then there is probably a risk of back pain and/or pain affecting the hand, arm or neck:

- repetitive or heavy lifting;
- bending and twisting;
- repeating an action too frequently;
- an uncomfortable working position;
- exerting too much force;
- working too long without breaks;
- an adverse working environment (eg hot or cold);
- intensive work, tight deadlines and lack of control over the work and working methods.

Manual handling

Employers must:

- avoid hazardous manual handling operations, so far as is reasonably practicable, eg carry out processes such as wrapping in the same place without handling the load;
- assess any hazardous manual handling operations that cannot be avoided, eg by using the 'MAC' (Manual handling assessment charts) – see 'Find out more';
- reduce the risk of injury so far as is reasonably practicable.

The law

The Manual Handling Operations Regulations 1992 (as amended in 2002) apply to work which involves lifting, lowering, pushing, pulling or carrying.

How can I reduce the risk?

Firstly does the job have to be done at all? If it does then consider if you can reduce the risk from manual handling.

Improve the task

- Use a lifting aid, such as a pallet truck, electric or hand-powered hoist, or a conveyor.
- Reduce the amount of twisting, stooping and reaching.
- Avoid lifting from floor level or above shoulder height, especially heavy loads.
- Reduce carrying distances.
- Avoid repetitive handling.
- Vary the work, allowing one set of muscles to rest while another is used.
- Push rather than pull.

Modify the load

Make the load:

- lighter or less bulky;
- easier to grasp;
- more stable;
- less damaging to hold, eg with no sharp edges.

If the load comes in from elsewhere, ask the supplier to help, eg by providing handles or smaller packages.

Improve the working environment

- Remove obstructions to free movement.
- Provide better flooring, without bumps or slippery surfaces.
- Avoid steps and steep ramps.
- Prevent extremes of hot and cold.
- Improve lighting.
- Provide protective clothing or PPE that is less restrictive.
- Ensure your employees' clothing and footwear is suitable for their work.

Make sure you:

- pay particular attention to those who have a physical weakness or health problem;
- take extra care of pregnant workers;
- give your employees enough information, eg about the range of tasks they are likely to face;
- provide training relevant to the jobs being done;
- provide equipment that is suitable for the task;
- carry out planned maintenance, eg of trolleys and other handling aids, to prevent problems.

Repetitive handling

Reduce the risks from repetitive handling

- Reduce the levels of force required, eg by maintaining equipment and using lighter tools with well-designed handles.
- Reduce repetitive movements, eg by varying tasks, rotating jobs, using power-driven tools, reducing machine pace and introducing rest and recovery time.
- Get rid of awkward positions by changing the workstation or the work.
- Improve the working environment, eg with better lighting, and a more comfortable temperature.

Practical tips for good lifting technique

Think before lifting/handling. Plan the lift. Can handling aids be used? Where is the load going to be placed? Will help be needed with the load? Remove obstructions such as discarded wrapping materials. For a long lift, consider resting the load mid-way on a table or bench to change grip.

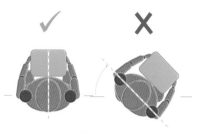

Avoid twisting the back or leaning sideways, especially while the back is bent. Shoulders should be kept level and facing in the same direction as the hips. Turning by moving the feet is better than twisting and lifting at the same time.

Keep the load close to the waist. The load should be kept close to the body for as long as possible while lifting. Keep the heaviest side of the load next to the body. If a close approach to the load is not possible, try to slide it towards the body before attempting to lift it.

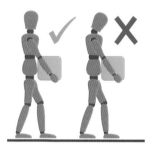

Adopt a stable position. The feet should be apart with one leg slightly forward to maintain balance (alongside the load, if it is on the ground). The worker should be prepared to move their feet during the lift to maintain their stability. Avoid tight clothing or unsuitable footwear, which may make this difficult.

Keep the head up when handling. Look ahead, not down at the load once it has been held securely.

Move smoothly. The load should not be jerked or snatched as this can make it harder to keep control and can increase the risk of injury.

Don't lift or handle more than can be easily managed. There is a difference between what people can lift and what they can safely lift. If in doubt, seek advice or get help.

Put down, then adjust. If precise positioning of the load is necessary, put it down first, then slide it into the desired position.

Get a good hold. Where possible the load should be hugged as close as possible to the body. This may be better than gripping it tightly with hands only.

Start in a good posture. At the start of the lift, slight bending of the back, hips and knees is preferable to fully flexing the back (stooping) or fully flexing the hips and knees (squatting).

Don't flex the back any further while lifting. This can happen if the legs begin to straighten before starting to raise the load.

HSE Infoline 0845 345 0055 **HSE website** www.hse.gov.uk **HSE Books** 01787 881165

12 Lifting and handling

Risk assessment guidelines for lifting and lowering

There is no such thing as a completely 'safe' manual handling operation, but working within the guideline figures in the following illustration will reduce the risk and the need for a more detailed assessment.

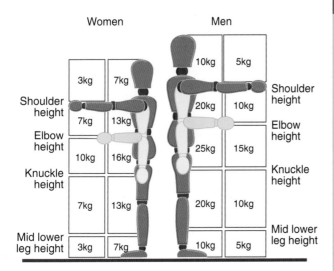

You can use it for:

- relatively infrequent tasks (less than 30 times per hour);
- tasks which do not involve twisting to the side;
- loads which can be easily held in both hands;
- operations which take place in reasonable working conditions.

In the illustration each box contains a guideline weight for lifting and lowering in that zone. The guideline weights are reduced if handling is done with the arms extended or at high or low levels, as that is where injuries are most likely.

- Observe the work activity you are assessing and compare it to the illustration. First, decide which box or boxes the lifter's hands pass through when moving the load. Then assess the maximum weight being handled. If it is less than the figure given in the box, the operation is within the guidelines.
- If the lifter's hands enter more than one box during the operation, use the smallest weight. Use an in-between weight if the hands are close to a boundary between boxes.

- The guideline weights are lower where the handler has to twist to the side during the operation, or for more frequent operations.

Find out more

Manual handling. Manual Handling Operations Regulations 1992 (as amended). Guidance on Regulations L23 (Third edition) ISBN 0 7176 2823 X

Upper limb disorders in the workplace HSG60 (Second edition) ISBN 0 7176 1978 8

Getting to grips with manual handling: A short guide Leaflet INDG143(rev2)

Aching arms (or RSI) in small businesses: Is ill health due to upper limb disorders a problem in your workplace? Leaflet INDG171(rev1)

Manual handling assessment charts Leaflet INDG383

Are you making the best use of lifting and handling aids? Leaflet INDG398

Visit www.hse.gov.uk/msd for more information on how to prevent back pain and how to carry out a manual handling assessment.

13

Noise

The hazards

Loud noise at work can damage your hearing and interferes with communication.

This hearing damage is usually gradual and it may only be when the damage caused by noise combines with hearing loss due to ageing that people realise how deaf they have become.

Hearing can also be damaged immediately by sudden, extremely loud noise.

You may also develop tinnitus, a distressing ringing, whistling, buzzing or humming in the ears.

Do you have a noise problem at work?

This will depend on how loud the noise is and how long people are exposed to it. If you can answer 'yes' to any of the following questions you will probably need to do something about the noise:

- Is the noise intrusive – like a busy street, a vacuum cleaner or a crowded restaurant – for most of the working day?
- Do your employees have to raise their voices to carry out a normal conversation when about 2 m apart for at least part of the day?
- Do your employees use noisy powered tools or machinery for more than half an hour each day?
- Do you work in a noisy industry, eg construction, demolition or road repair; woodworking; plastics processing; engineering; textile manufacture; general fabrication; forging, pressing or stamping; paper or board making; canning or bottling; foundries?
- Are there noises due to impacts (such as hammering, drop forging, pneumatic impact tools etc), explosive sources such as cartridge-operated tools or detonators, or guns?

Noise action and limit values

Noise is measured in decibels (dB). The action levels are defined in terms of daily noise exposure (the average over the working day), and peak noise exposure (sudden noises).

The 'lower exposure action values' are 80 dB for daily exposure and 135 dB for peak noise. The 'upper exposure action values' are 85 dB for daily exposure and 137 dB for peak noise.

The limits, which must not be exceeded, are 87 dB for daily exposure, and 140 dB for peak noise – but note that in checking whether the limits have been exceeded, you can account for the effect of any hearing protection being worn.

The law

The Control of Noise at Work Regulations 2005 (in force from 6 April 2006) require employers to take action to prevent or reduce risks to health and safety from exposure to noise at work. They also define action levels, where specific additional actions are required, and limit values, which must not be exceeded.

43

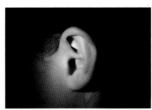

What do I need to do?

Start with a risk assessment which should:

- identify who is at risk from noise, and why;
- contain a reliable estimate of those people's noise exposure;
- identify what you need to do to comply with the law, eg whether noise-control measures or hearing protection are needed, and which employees need to have health surveillance.

Make sure you use reliable data which is representative of how your employees work and how it may vary from day to day, eg from measurements in your own workplace, information from workplaces similar to yours, or from suppliers of machinery.

Record the findings of your risk assessment and record in an action plan anything you identify as being necessary to comply with the law, setting out what you have done and what you are going to do.

How do I control the risks from noise?

Wherever there are risks from noise you should be looking for ways of controlling them, and you should always be keeping up with good practice and standards for noise control within your industry.

Where there are things that you can do to reduce risks, that are reasonably practicable, they should be done.

Where exposures are likely to be at or above the upper action values, your noise-control measures must be part of a planned programme.

There are many ways of reducing noise and noise exposure – often a combination of methods work best. First think about how to remove the loud noise altogether. If that is not possible, do all you can to control the noise at source. Take measures to protect individual workers if you need to. Consider the following:

- Use a different, quieter process or quieter equipment, and maybe introduce a low-noise purchasing policy for machinery and equipment.
- Introduce engineering controls, eg fit silencers to air exhausts and blowing nozzles.
- Modify the paths by which the noise travels through the air to the people exposed, eg erect enclosures around machines.
- Design and lay out the workplace for low noise emission, eg use absorptive materials such as open cell foam or mineral wool within the building to reduce reflected sound.
- Limit the time spent in noisy areas – every halving of the time spent in a noisy area will reduce noise exposure by 3 dB.

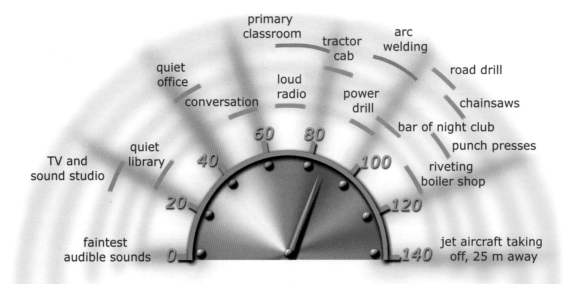

HSE Infoline 0845 345 0055 HSE website www.hse.gov.uk HSE Books 01787 881165

Hearing protection

Hearing protection (earmuffs or earplugs) should be issued to employees:

- where extra protection is needed above what can be achieved using noise control;
- as a short-term measure while other methods of controlling noise are being developed.

Do not use hearing protection as an alternative to controlling noise by the technical and organisational methods described earlier.

What do I have to do about hearing protection?

You must:

- provide your employees with hearing protectors if they ask for them and their noise exposure is between the lower and upper exposure action values;
- provide your employees with hearing protectors and make sure they use them properly when their noise exposure exceeds the upper exposure action values;
- identify hearing protection zones, ie areas where the use of hearing protection is compulsory, and mark them with signs if possible;
- provide your employees with training and information on how to use and care for the hearing protectors;
- ensure the hearing protectors are properly used and maintained.

How can I make sure hearing protection is used effectively?

- Make sure the protectors give enough protection – aim at least to get below 85 dB at the ear.
- Target the use of protectors to the noisy tasks and jobs in a working day.
- Select protectors which are suitable for the working environment – consider how comfortable and hygienic they are.
- Think about how they will be worn with other protective equipment, eg hard hats, dust masks and eye protection.
- Provide a range of protectors so that employees can choose ones which suit them.
- Do not provide protectors which cut out too much noise – this can cause isolation, or lead to an unwillingness to wear them.
- Do not make the use of hearing protection compulsory where the law doesn't require it.
- Do not have a 'blanket' approach to hearing protection – it is better to target its use and only encourage people to wear it when they need to.

HSE Infoline 0845 345 0055   HSE website www.hse.gov.uk   HSE Books 01787 881165

Health surveillance (hearing checks)

You must provide regular hearing checks in controlled conditions for all your employees who are likely to be regularly exposed above the upper exposure action values, or are at risk for any other reason. The purpose of this is to:

- warn you when employees might be suffering from early signs of hearing damage;
- give you the opportunity to do something to prevent the damage getting worse;
- check control measures are working.

Large companies may have access to in-house occupational health services to arrange health surveillance. Where there are no facilities in-house you will need to use an external contractor.

Find out more

Controlling noise at work. The Control of Noise at Work Regulations 2005. Guidance on Regulations L108 (Second edition) ISBN 0 7176 6164 4

Noise at work: Guidance for employers on the Control of Noise at Work Regulations 2005 Leaflet INDG362(rev1)

Protect your hearing or lose it! Pocket card INDG363(rev1)

Visit www.hse.gov.uk/noise for more information and advice on noise control and noise risk assessment.

Vibration

The hazards

Frequent and regular exposure to hand-arm vibration from hand-held power tools such as chipping hammers, grinders and chainsaws, and other machinery, can cause hand-arm vibration syndrome (HAVS). This is a painful and disabling condition which affects the nerves, blood vessels, muscles and joints of the hands and arms. It causes tingling and numbness in the fingers, reduces the sense of touch, and affects the blood circulation (vibration white finger).

Whole-body vibration mainly affects drivers of vehicles used off-road, such as dumpers, excavators, tractors and some lift trucks. It is associated mostly with low back pain. However, back pain can also be caused by other factors, such as manual handling and postural strains, and while exposure to vibration and shocks may be painful for people with back problems, it will not necessarily be the cause of the problem.

What do I need to do?

Employers are required by the Regulations to introduce a formal programme of control measures when employees are exposed above a daily exposure action value, and to prevent employees from being exposed above a daily exposure limit value. You must also provide information, training and appropriate health surveillance for any employees judged to be at risk.

Reduce hand-arm vibration

- Identify hazardous machines, tools and processes, especially those which cause tingling or numbness in the hands after a few minutes' use.
- Do the job another way without using high-vibration tools if possible.
- Ask about likely vibration levels for the way you use equipment before deciding which new tool or machine to buy or hire.
- Provide suitable tools designed to cut down vibration.
- Make sure people use the right tool for the job and are trained to use it correctly.
- Make sure tools are maintained to prevent vibration increasing – check the sharpness of tools, the condition of abrasive wheels, and anti-vibration mounts where fitted.
- Maintain machines as recommended by the manufacturer.
- Check whether the job can be altered to reduce the grip or pressure needed.

The law

The Control of Vibration at Work Regulations 2005 came into force on 6 July 2005. The Regulations require employers to assess and control the risks to their employees from exposure to hand-arm and whole-body vibration.

HSE Infoline 0845 345 0055 **HSE website** www.hse.gov.uk **HSE Books** 01787 881165

14 Vibration

Reduce whole-body vibration

- Choose vehicles or machines designed to cope with the task and conditions.
- Keep site roadways level, fill in potholes and remove debris.
- Train drivers to operate machines and attachments smoothly, to drive at appropriate speeds for the ground conditions and to adjust suspension seats correctly.
- Maintain and repair machine and vehicle suspension systems, tyre pressures and suspension seats.

Find out more

Hand-arm vibration. The Control of Vibration at Work Regulations 2005. Guidance on Regulations L140 ISBN 0 7176 6125 3

Whole-body vibration. The Control of Vibration at Work Regulations 2005. Guidance on Regulations L141 ISBN 0 7176 6126 1

Control the risks from hand-arm vibration: Advice for employers on the Control of Vibration at Work Regulations 2005 Leaflet INDG175(rev2)

Control back-pain risks from whole-body vibration: Advice for employers on the Control of Vibration at Work Regulations 2005 Leaflet INDG242(rev1)

Hand-arm vibration: Advice for employees Pocket card INDG296(rev1)

Drive away bad backs: Advice for mobile machine operators and drivers Pocket card INDG404

Visit www.hse.gov.uk/vibration for more information and online tools for calculating vibration exposure.

HSE Infoline 0845 345 0055 HSE website www.hse.gov.uk HSE Books 01787 881165

Electricity

The hazards

The three main hazards are contact with live parts, fire and explosion. Each year about 1000 accidents at work involving shock and burn are reported and about 25 of these are fatal. Fires started by poor electrical installations and faulty electrical equipment cause many other deaths and injuries. Explosions are caused by electrical apparatus or static electricity igniting flammable vapours or dusts.

Remember that normal mains voltage (230 volts AC) can kill. The risks are greatest when electricity is used in harsh conditions, eg portable electrical equipment used outdoors, or in cramped spaces with a lot of earthed metalwork, eg inside a boiler, air cupboard or bin.

Before you start

Assess the risks from electricity in your workplace and use the precautions here to control them.

Reduce the voltage

- Lighting can run at 12 or 25 volts.
- Portable tools can run at 110 volts from an isolating transformer.

Provide and keep a safe installation

- Provide enough socket outlets, if necessary, by using a multi-plug socket block – overloading sockets by using adapters can cause a fire.
- Fuses, circuit-breakers and other devices must be correctly rated for the circuit they protect.
- There must be a switch or isolator near each fixed machine to cut off power in an emergency.
- The mains switches must be readily accessible and clearly identified.
- Any new electrical installation must be properly designed, installed and tested safely with regard to appropriate standards.
- Ensure that the installation and equipment is maintained.

The law

Look at the Electricity at Work Regulations 1989 for the full requirements.

HSE Infoline 0845 345 0055 HSE website www.hse.gov.uk HSE Books 01787 881165

Provide insulation, protection and earthing

- Power cables to machines must be insulated and protected from damage, eg sheathed and armoured or installed in conduit. Earth connections must be in good condition.
- If you use a flexible cable you must always use a proper plug with the flex firmly clamped to stop the wires (particularly the earth) pulling out of the terminals.
- Some tools are double insulated for extra protection and these have only two wires (neutral and live). Make sure you connect them properly.
- You must ensure cables, plugs, sockets and fittings are robust enough and adequately protected for the working environment.
- Replace frayed and damaged cables completely. Join lengths in good condition only by using proper connectors or cable couplers.
- A residual current device can act as a safety trip when there is a fault. This is not a substitute for a proper installation.

- Protect light bulbs, or other items which may be easily damaged in use.
- You must use special protection where electrical equipment is used in flammable or dusty environments. Low-voltage equipment (eg 12 volts) gives no protection against igniting flammable vapours. To choose the correct equipment you may need specialist advice (see Chapter 18 for further details).
- When carrying or pouring organic powders (eg flour, tea dust) or flammable liquids, use closed metal containers and make sure all metalwork is bonded and earthed.
- For jobs like electrostatic paint spraying, make sure both the work and anyone in the area are adequately earthed, eg by getting the operator and others to wear anti-static footwear, otherwise electrostatic charges can build up which can cause a spark.

HSE Infoline 0845 345 0055 HSE website www.hse.gov.uk HSE Books 01787 881165

Safe operation

You must ensure all your electrical equipment is safe for people to use, including equipment that is used away from your premises. Employees should know how to use electrical equipment safely. You must not allow anyone to work on or near live equipment, unless it is unavoidable and special precautions are taken. Ask your inspector for advice.

Check that:

- suspect or faulty equipment is taken out of use, labelled 'Do not use' and kept secure until checked by a competent person;
- tools and power sockets are switched off before plugging in or unplugging;
- appliances are unplugged before cleaning or making adjustments.

Overhead electric lines

Contact with overhead electric lines accounts for half of the fatal electrical accidents each year. Electricity can flash over from overhead power lines even though plant and equipment may not touch them.

Don't work under them where any equipment (eg ladders, a crane jib, a tipper lorry body, a scaffold pole) could come within a minimum of 6 m of a power line without seeking advice. Consult the line owner, eg your local electricity company or railway company.

Maintenance

All electrical equipment, including portable appliances, wiring installations, generators or battery sets and everything connected to them, must be maintained to prevent danger.

This means carrying out checks and inspections and repairing and testing as necessary – how often will depend on the equipment you use and where you use it. You may find it helpful to keep records of inspection and combined inspection and testing.

Don't forget hired or borrowed tools or equipment that employees may bring in (eg mains-powered radios) or equipment like floor polishers which may be used after the premises have closed.

- You must prevent access to electrical danger by keeping isolator and fuse-box covers closed and (if possible) locked, with the key held by a responsible person.
- Anyone carrying out electrical work must be competent to do it safely, which may mean bringing in outside contractors. If you do this, make sure they belong to a body which checks their work, such as the National Inspection Council for Electrical Installation Contracting (NICEIC).
- Anyone carrying out repairs to electrical equipment or installations should ensure that the equipment or installation is dead and has been suitably isolated (eg by locking off the supply).
- Check that residual current circuit-breakers work by operating the test button regularly.
- Make sure that special maintenance requirements of waterproof or explosion-protected equipment have been written down and that someone is made responsible for carrying out the work without damaging the protection.

HSE Infoline 0845 345 0055 HSE website www.hse.gov.uk HSE Books 01787 881165

Electric shock

Would you know what to do if someone received an electric shock?

Knowing what to do should be part of your emergency procedures and first-aid arrangements (see Chapter 25). Think about displaying a copy of the 'Electric shock' poster, which shows you what to do.

Underground cables

- Consult your local electricity company if you are likely to be digging near buried cables – they should know where these are.
- Always assume cables will be present when digging holes in the street, pavement or near buildings.
- If you have to work near services, use service plans, locators and safe digging practice to avoid danger.

Find out more

Memorandum of guidance on the Electricity at Work Regulations 1989. Guidance on Regulations HSR25 ISBN 0 7176 1602 9

Avoiding danger from underground services HSG47 (Second edition) ISBN 0 7176 1744 0

Electricity at work: Safe working practices HSG85 (Second edition) ISBN 0 7176 2164 2

Electrical safety on construction sites HSG141 ISBN 0 7176 1000 4

Avoidance of danger from overhead electric powerlines General Guidance Note GS6 (Third edition) ISBN 0 7176 1348 8

Electric shock: First-aid procedures Poster ISBN 0 7176 6195 4

Electrical safety and you Leaflet INDG231

Visit www.hse.gov.uk/electricity for more information

Radiations

The hazards

Visible light is just one part of the spectrum of electro-magnetic radiation, which ranges from electromagnetic fields (EMFs) and radio waves at one end to ultraviolet (UV) light and gamma rays at the other.

Ionising radiations:

- X-rays, gamma rays and particulate radiation from radiation generators, some high-voltage equipment, radiography equipment, radiography containers, substance gauges and radioactive substances, including radon gas.

Non-ionising radiations:

- radio frequency and microwaves from, eg plastics welding, some communications, catering, drying and heating equipment;
- infra-red from any glowing source, eg glass and metal production, and some lasers;
- visible radiation from all high-intensity visible light sources, and high-intensity beams, such as from some lasers;
- ultraviolet (UV) from, eg welding, some lasers, mercury vapour lamps, carbon arcs, the sun.

Before you start

- Try to reduce any exposures to ionising and UV radiation as far as possible.
- Where the hazard arises from the process or the equipment you use, you may be able to use something safer, eg ultrasonic non-destructive testing instead of X-rays.
- Check on any radiation hazards at the time of purchase.

Ionising radiations

- Can cause burns, dermatitis, cancer, cell damage or blood changes and cataracts.
- Permission to store and dispose of radioactive substances is given by the Environment Agency (the Scottish Environment Protection Agency in Scotland and the Environment Agency in Wales). Also see the Radioactive Substances Act 1993.
- IRR 99 also applies where the naturally occurring gas radon is present above a defined level.
- Contractors carrying out site radiography (eg checking welds on pipework or vessels) must notify HSE on each occasion before work starts (see www.hse.gov.uk/radiation/ionising/indradiography.htm).
- Smoke detectors and static eliminators often contain radioactive sources. Find out the rules for safe storage and use from the supplier and never tamper with them.
- Treat luminous articles and self-illuminating devices with similar respect.

The law

The Ionising Radiations Regulations 1999 (IRR 99) apply to most work with ionising radiations, including exposure to naturally occurring radon gas. They also apply to the protection of outside workers, eg contractors. This chapter also gives advice on complying with the general legal duties when dealing with non-ionising radiations. Legislation is being developed to transpose EU Directives on EMFs and optical radiation safety into national law. HSE currently advises employers to use the recommendations of the International Commission on Non-Ionizing Radiation Protection (see www.icnirp.org) as the basis for assessing the risks arising from exposures to EMFs, UV, infra-red and optical radiation.

If your work with ionising radiations could produce a radiation emergency (ie an event that could lead to a member of the public receiving a dose of ionising radiation above certain levels) the Radiation (Emergency Preparedness and Public Information) Regulations 2001 (REPPIR) may also apply.

16 Radiations

You may need to:

- appoint a radiation protection adviser and one or more of your employees to supervise radiation work;
- arrange for medical examination/reviews and routine dose assessments of employees who you designate as 'classified persons'. Make arrangements (contingency plans) to cater for spills of radioactive substances, X-ray exposures failing to terminate etc;
- arrange for tests where raised levels of radon gas are likely because of workplace location, construction and ventilation. Have any necessary improvements carried out.

Microwaves and radio frequencies

- Can cause heating of any exposed parts of the body.
- Leakage of energy from microwave ovens is normally very small. Control it by keeping door seals clean and ensuring that the hinges, door latch and safety interlocks all work.
- Reduce exposure to stray radio frequency (RF) energy from heaters, driers and presses by shielding the applicator electrodes. Limit exposure time or avoid getting too close to the source.
- Do not touch RF electrodes. Prevent unauthorised access to the high-voltage electrical equipment, eg by interlocking all cubicle doors.

Infra-red

- Can cause burns and cataracts.
- Protective clothing may be needed to reduce warming, burning and irritation of the skin from some 'hot bodies' such as pools of molten metal. Eye protection with suitable filters should be worn to avoid discomfort. This is essential with some infra-red sources, such as certain lasers (see Chapter 24).

Ultraviolet (UV)

- Can cause sunburn, conjunctivitis, arc eye, skin cancer, production of toxic levels of ozone.
- UV sources in equipment should normally be in an enclosure, or screened.
- Take care to avoid exposures to UV light, eg by wearing suitable clothing and eye protection.
- During welding use special goggles or a face screen and protect passers-by, eg with screens.
- When fitting replacement UV lamps, choose the correct type specified by the manufacturer. Filters should be kept in place at all times and replaced after changing bulbs or if they are damaged.
- Insect-killing devices with bright blue light sources are often found in food premises and are not harmful to the eyes in normal use. However people must not be exposed to germicidal UV lamps used to sterilise surfaces.

Lasers

- Can cause heating and photochemical injury of eye or skin tissue.
- A laser, a concentrated beam of radiation, which may not always be visible, can be dangerous whether it is viewed directly or after reflection from a smooth surface.
- Maintenance workers who have to examine inside machines may be most at risk. They need to be trained and follow a work system, which may include the use of eye protection.
- High-powered lasers should normally be inside a safety-interlocked enclosure – only use them after taking expert advice. Do not over-ride any interlocks.
- Where lasers are used for display, eg at bars, nightclubs or stage shows and performances, there could be risks to the public – seek expert advice (see HSE's guidance book HSG95).

Find out more

Work with ionising radiation. Ionising Radiations Regulations 1999. Approved Code of Practice and guidance L121 ISBN 0 7176 1746 7

A guide to the Radiation (Emergency Preparedness and Public Information) Regulations 2001. Guidance on Regulations L126 ISBN 0 7176 2240 1

The radiation safety of lasers used for display purposes HSG95 ISBN 0 7176 0691 0

Visit www.hse.gov.uk/radiation/index.htm for information on both ionising and non-ionising radiation.

Harmful substances

The hazards

Many materials you work with contain substances that can harm your health. They may be dusts, gases or fumes that you breathe in. They may be liquids or powders that come into contact with your eyes or skin. Harmful substances can be present in anything from paints and cleaners through to flour dust and diesel fume.

The harmful effects can either be immediate such as dizziness or stinging eyes, or can take many years to slowly develop such as damage to your lungs. Most of the long-term effects cannot be cured once they develop. Some substances may cause asthma and many can damage the skin.

Special care is needed when handling cancer-causing substances (carcinogens).

Chapter 18 covers flammable and explosive substances, while radiation hazards are dealt with in Chapter 16. Chapter 19 gives advice about watching out for possible symptoms of ill health.

What you need to do

Where you use something which might cause harm, you must assess the risks to health and put in place measures to control those risks.

This chapter will help you carry out the assessment. It will help you decide whether your controls are adequate and what changes, if any, you need to make.

First of all find out information about the materials you use. The contents and hazards of the product must be indicated on the package or label. The supplier must also provide accurate and complete safety data sheets.

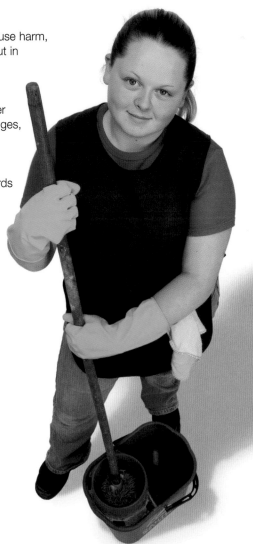

The law

If you use substances which might cause harm, look at the Control of Substances Hazardous to Health Regulations (COSHH) 2002 (as amended), the Control of Lead at Work Regulations 2002 and the Control of Asbestos at Work Regulations 2002 for the full requirements.

If you are a supplier look at the Chemicals (Hazard Information and Packaging for Supply) Regulations 2002 (as amended) and the Carriage of Dangerous Goods and Use of Transportable Pressure Equipment Regulations 2004 (as amended 2005) (the Carriage Regulations 2004).

If you manufacture or import new chemicals, look at the Notification of New Substances (Amendment) Regulations 2002.

Are your controls adequate?

There are various ways of deciding. Probably the simplest way is to use this chart from the COSHH Regulations.

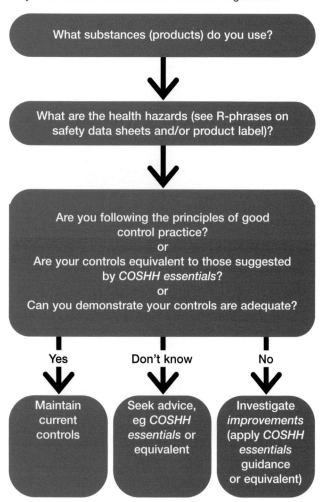

For many harmful substances and processes there is guidance available on good control practice from trade and industry associations and suppliers, as well as HSE.

You may also be able to use the simple step-by-step advice from HSE's *COSHH essentials*, which is freely available on HSE's website (www.coshh-essentials.org.uk/).

You could carry out an assessment to establish how likely it is that ill health can be caused by the substances in your workplace.

Carry out an assessment

To do this you need to consider:

■ the hazards of substances or their ingredients – read the labels and safety data sheets. If in doubt contact your supplier. Remember that some hazardous substances can be produced by the process you use, eg wood dust from sanding;

■ the route into the body (breathed in, swallowed or taken in through the skin) and the result of exposure by each of these routes;

■ the concentration or conditions likely to cause ill health;

■ the first symptoms of over-exposure and whether exposure could result in ill-health effects, eg asthma or dermatitis;

■ who could be exposed. Don't forget maintenance workers, contractors and members of the public;

■ if people could be exposed accidentally, eg while cleaning, through spillage or if your controls fail;

■ how often people work with, or are exposed to, the substance;

■ how much people work with and for how long.

Control measures

Do you really need to use a particular substance? Can you use a safer material or change the process to avoid its use? If not, you must provide adequate control measures. 'Control measure' means any measure taken to reduce exposure. This includes:

■ changing the process to reduce risks;
■ containment;
■ systems of work;
■ cleaning;
■ ventilation;
■ personal protective equipment.

You may need more than one control measure. Use the combination which will be most effective and reliable. You will also need to supervise and check that your controls are still working.

Change the process to reduce risks

- Reduce the temperature of the process to reduce the amount of vapour getting into the air.
- Use pellets instead of powders as they are less dusty.
- Minimise leakage, eg of powder from equipment to reduce the spread of contamination.
- Reduce the amount used, the number of people exposed, and how long they are exposed for.

Containment

- Enclose the process or activity as much as possible to minimise the escape or release of the harmful substance.
- Use closed transfer and handling systems and minimise handling of materials.

Systems of work to reduce exposure

- Plan the storage of materials and use appropriate containers.
- Only store the minimum required for your production needs.
- Correctly label stores and containers.
- Separate incompatible materials, eg acids and caustics.
- Plan the storage and disposal of waste.

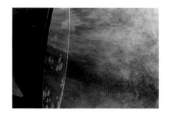

Cleaning

- Have the right equipment to hand to clear up spillages quickly and safely.
- Plan and organise the workplace so that it is easily and effectively cleaned.
- Have smooth work surfaces to allow easy cleaning.
- Clean regularly using a 'dust free' method – vacuum, don't sweep.

Local exhaust ventilation

Use a properly designed local exhaust ventilation (LEV) (extraction) system which sucks dust, fume, gases or vapour through a hood or booth and reduces the exposure of the worker.

An effective extraction system will:

- be usable by the worker;
- enclose the process as much as possible;
- be powerful enough to capture or contain the harmful substance;
- be positioned to receive the harmful substance from the process;
- filter and discharge the air to a safe place;
- be robust enough to withstand the process and work environment;
- have been tested to check that it works.

Common errors in applying extraction are:

- the effectiveness of small hoods is usually overestimated – be realistic;
- the hood is usually too far away from the process;
- the hood doesn't surround the process enough;
- inadequate airflow;
- failure to check that the extraction continues to work;
- workers are not consulted, extraction gets in the way and is therefore unusable.

General ventilation

- All workplaces need an adequate supply of fresh air.
- General ventilation usually means using a fan to blow air into the workroom.
- Sometimes planned, powered general ventilation is an integral part of a set of control measures, eg the welding of large fabrications in a workshop.

Welfare facilities

Provide good washing and changing facilities. See Chapter 2 for more general requirements.

Personal protective clothing and equipment

Where adequate control of exposure cannot be achieved by other means, provide personal protective clothing and equipment, in combination with other control measures. Don't jump straight to personal protective equipment (PPE). It is not as reliable or effective as other measures. Chapter 24 gives further advice.

Maintain controls

All elements of your control measures must be checked and reviewed regularly to make sure they continue to be effective. These checks should be adequate to determine whether improvements are required and will include:

■ maintaining plant and equipment – all ventilation equipment must be examined and tested regularly by a competent person. This may involve measuring the air speed or the pressures in the system, or air sampling in the workroom. In general, all LEV must be examined and tested every 14 months;

■ making sure systems of work are being followed and revising them if they're not working;
■ making sure personal protective equipment is suitable, properly fitted and maintained.

In special cases you may need to arrange health surveillance (see Chapter 19).

You may need advice, particularly for potentially serious risks and/or difficult-to-control processes, from someone who is competent in that area of work, eg an occupational hygienist. Visit the website of the British Occupational Hygiene Society: www.bohs.org.uk for more information.

Simple checks to control dust and mist

Fine dust and mist is invisible in normal lighting. You can make it visible with a 'dust lamp'. Any bright torch will do. Observe the dust/mist by looking down the beam towards the torch.

■ Note the settlement and spread of contamination on surfaces.
■ Check the gauge or tell-tale indicator on the extraction system.
■ Check for damage and leakage from the process.
■ Speak to the operator and encourage reporting of any defects.

Workplace exposure limits

As well as following the principles of good practice for the control of exposure to substances hazardous to health, you need to be aware that, for many substances, limits have been set on the amounts of substances that workers are permitted to breathe.

These limits are known as workplace exposure limits (WELs). They are listed in HSE's booklet EH40 *Workplace exposure limits*. If the substance is known to cause cancer or asthma (check the label/safety data sheet), you must control exposure to as low a level as reasonably practicable.

Record and review

Except in very simple cases, you should keep a record of what you have found out about the risks to health and the appropriate control measures and when they will be implemented and by whom. Write down:

■ where exposures occur;
■ what the control measures are;
■ how you will maintain control.

Keep an eye on things. Changes in equipment, materials or methods may require you to review your earlier decisions. In any case each year review the risks and control measures.

Information and training

You should tell workers:

■ the hazards;
■ how they could be affected;
■ what to do to keep themselves and others safe, ie how the risks are to be controlled;
■ how to use control measures, including personal protective equipment and the correct systems of work;
■ how to check and spot when things are going wrong and who to report them to;
■ the results of any exposure monitoring or health surveillance;
■ about emergency procedures (see Chapter 25).

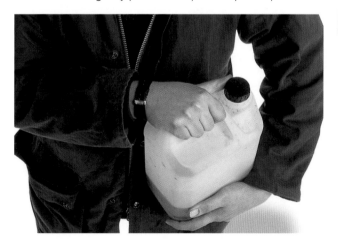

Asbestos

Asbestos has been widely used, eg as lagging on plant and pipework, in insulation products such as fireproofing panels, in asbestos cement roofing materials, and as sprayed coating on structural steelwork to insulate against fire and noise.

All types of asbestos can be dangerous if disturbed. The danger only arises when asbestos fibres become airborne and are breathed in. Exposure can cause diseases such as lung cancer.

If you are responsible for the maintenance and repair of your work premises, you must find out if there is any asbestos and where it is. If you cannot do this, presume that it exists. You will need to manage any risks from the asbestos and let anyone who may disturb it know where it is and what condition it is in. Well-sealed, undamaged asbestos is best left alone.

You will then need to inspect the condition of asbestos-containing material on a regular basis. If it begins to show signs of deterioration and is liable to give off dust, you may need to have it removed.

If you have to work on asbestos you must:

- carry out an assessment of the risks to the health of employees from exposure to asbestos;
- use the working methods and precautions described in the asbestos Approved Codes of Practice, or other equally safe methods such as those detailed in HSE's *Asbestos essentials task manual*.

Asbestos has its own regulations:

- All work with asbestos and the precautions needed are covered by the Control of Asbestos at Work Regulations 2002.
- The Asbestos (Licensing) Regulations 1983, as amended in 1998, prohibit contractors working on asbestos insulation, asbestos board or asbestos coating unless they have a licence issued by HSE. This does not include asbestos cement sheets.
- The Asbestos (Prohibitions) Regulations 1992, as amended in 1999, prohibit the import, supply (including second-hand articles) and use of all types of asbestos.

Products containing asbestos must carry a warning label.

Find out more

Work with asbestos which does not normally require a licence. Control of Asbestos at Work Regulations 2002. Approved Code of Practice and guidance L27 (Fourth edition) ISBN 0 7176 2562 1

Work with asbestos insulation, asbestos coating and asbestos insulating board. Control of Asbestos at Work Regulations 2002. Approved Code of Practice and guidance L28 (Fourth edition) ISBN 0 7176 2563 X

The management of asbestos in non-domestic premises. Regulation 4 of the Control of Asbestos at Work Regulations 2002. Approved Code of Practice and guidance L127 ISBN 0 7176 2382 3

Asbestos essentials task manual: Task guidance sheets for the building maintenance and allied trades HSG210 ISBN 0 7176 1887 0

A short guide to managing asbestos in premises Leaflet INDG223(rev3)

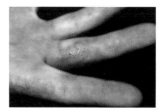

Lead

Work which exposes people to lead or its compounds is covered by the Control of Lead at Work Regulations 2002 and an Approved Code of Practice (see 'Find out more'). Risks may arise when lead dust or fume is breathed in; powder, dust, paint or paste swallowed; or compounds taken in through the skin.

As well as obvious work such as high temperature melting, making batteries or repairing radiators, there may be risks from repair or demolition of structures which have been painted with lead-based paints.

You must assess the risk and where necessary provide control of the process, protective clothing, air sampling and health surveillance.

If you work with lead it is advisable to discuss the work with your inspectors and HSE's Employment Medical Advisory Service (EMAS). Contact HSE's Infoline for details.

Find out more

Control of lead at work. Control of Lead at Work Regulations 2002. Approved Code of Practice and guidance L132 (Third edition) ISBN 0 7176 2565 6

Lead and you: A guide to working safely with lead Leaflet INDG305

Skin disease

Skin disease, including dermatitis, may be caused by contact with chemicals in the materials you work with, such as cutting oils, thinners and resins. Abrasives, dust and wet work can also cause dermatitis which can be seriously disfiguring and disabling and may affect your ability to work.

Good practice

- Read the labels on containers to find out if the material can cause skin disease.
- Design the work process and organise the work to minimise skin contact with the material, eg reduce leakage, spray and spread and have facilities to clear up spills etc. Select the right gloves.
- Train workers to properly wear gloves, including putting them on and taking them off without contaminating themselves.
- Where appropriate select suitable pre-work skin cream.
- Provide adequate washing facilities including warm water, soap and dry towels.
- Provide after-work moisturising cream.
- Provide first-aid facilities for minor cuts.
- Keep any cuts covered.
- Arrange for a responsible person to check skin regularly.
- Draw up clear instructions.
- Supervise workers to ensure your systems of work are followed.

17 Harmful substances

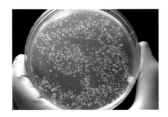

Bacteria and viruses

Bacteria and viruses can:

■ infect the body when they are breathed in, swallowed, or when they penetrate the skin;
■ cause allergic reactions.

The hazards

■ Legionnaires' disease – the bacteria causing this can be found in many recirculating water systems such as cooling towers, sprays and showers.
■ Water-borne infections such as leptospirosis (Weil's disease). This is associated with rats, but can be spread by cattle, and may affect, eg farmers, water industry workers and people involved in water sports.
■ Infections through blood contact – a risk in, eg hairdressing, tattooing, health care.
■ Diseases transmitted by living or dead animals, eg to farmers, pet show workers.
■ Diseases from people – a risk, eg for health care workers.

Most biological risks can be reduced by simple control methods. Sometimes immunisation may be needed. If you are in an 'at risk' group seek advice from HSE's Employment Medical Advisory Service (EMAS). Contact HSE's Infoline for details.

Find out more

Control of substances hazardous to health (Fifth edition). The Control of Substances Hazardous to Health Regulations 2002 (as amended). Approved Code of Practice and guidance L5 (Fifth edition) ISBN 0 7176 2981 3

Legionnaires' disease. The control of legionella bacteria in water systems. Approved Code of Practice and guidance L8 (Third edition) ISBN 0 7176 1772 6

Maintenance, examination and testing of local exhaust ventilation HSG54 (Second edition) ISBN 0 7176 1485 9

EH40/2005 Workplace exposure limits: Containing the list of workplace exposure limits for use with the Control of Substances Hazardous to Health Regulations 2002 (as amended) Environmental Hygiene Guidance Note EH40 (2005) ISBN 0 7176 2977 5 (updated annually)

Respiratory sensitisers and COSHH: Breathe freely – An employers' leaflet on preventing occupational asthma Leaflet INDG95(rev2)

COSHH a brief guide to the Regulations: What you need to know about the Control of Substances Hazardous to Health Regulations 2002 (COSHH) Leaflet INDG136(rev3)

Preventing dermatitis at work: Advice for employers and employees Leaflet INDG233

Flammable and explosive substances

The hazards

Some gases, liquids and solids can cause explosions or fire.

Common materials may burn violently at high temperature in oxygen-rich conditions, eg when a gas cylinder is leaking.

Some dusts form a cloud which will explode when ignited. A small explosion can disturb dust and create a second explosion severe enough to destroy a building.

Serious explosions can occur in plant such as ovens, stoves and boilers (see Chapter 9).

Some materials are explosives and need special precautions and licensing arrangements.

Some flammable liquids and substances are also corrosive or toxic and may pose risks to health (see Chapter 17).

Before you start

The supplier's safety data sheet will help you decide how to handle flammable and explosive substances.

Think about the following:

- Do the job another way.
- Use liquids with higher flash points. Look at the data sheets – remember a high flash point is safer than a low one.
- Reduce the amounts you keep on site.
- Check with the supplier about any special precautions which may be needed when certain materials are delivered in bulk.
- Check container labels and consignment notes to make sure that goods are supplied as ordered.

The law

The Dangerous Substances and Explosive Atmospheres Regulations 2002 (DSEAR) require you to carry out a risk assessment of any work activities involving dangerous substances so that you can eliminate or reduce any risks identified.

If you operate a petrol filling station you need a licence under the Petroleum Acts.

If you are a supplier look at the Chemicals (Hazard Information and Packaging for Supply) Regulations 2002 (as amended) and the Carriage of Dangerous Goods and Use of Transportable Pressure Equipment Regulations 2004 (as amended 2005) (the Carriage Regulations 2004).

If you manufacture or import new chemicals, look at the Notification of New Substances (Amendment) Regulations 2002.

Explosives

- Specific control is applied to most explosives, including fireworks and safety cartridges. You may need a licence or other permit – contact your inspector for advice.
- Some substances like organic peroxide and other oxidisers can explode if they are not stored and handled properly. Check labels and safety data sheets.

Storage

Some chemicals react dangerously together. Such classes of material should be stored correctly, eg oxidising substances should be kept apart from flammable ones.

Use the information from the supplier and the package label to decide storage arrangements. Materials can be separated by distance, by a physical barrier or (sometimes) by other non-reactive materials.

Good storage will:

- be separate from process areas (where fire or leakage is more likely);
- be in a safe, well-ventilated place, isolated from buildings;
- prevent incompatible chemicals being mixed, eg by spillage, damage to packaging or by wetting during firefighting;
- reduce the risk of damage, eg by lift truck, and by ensuring that cylinders are secured and stored upright;
- prevent rapid spread of fire or smoke, or liquid or molten substances, eg by the store being made of fire-resisting material;
- exclude sources of ignition, eg static electricity, unprotected electrical equipment, cigarettes and naked flames;
- include empty drums or cylinders as well as full ones – the risk can be just as great.

Housekeeping

- Remove grease frequently from ducts, such as kitchen ventilators and cooker extractor hoods.
- Keep the workplace tidy and free from old containers etc. Plastic foam crumb and off-cuts are a particular hazard.
- Contaminated clothing or containers need careful disposal.
- Keep flammable waste secure from vandals.

Flammable liquids

- The safest place to store any flammable liquids and substances is in a separate building or in a safe place in the open air.
- If highly flammable liquids have to be stored inside workrooms you should store as little as possible and they should be kept on their own in a special metal cupboard or bin.
- Larger stocks should be held in a fire-resisting store with spillage retention and good ventilation.

If you run a factory you should:

- minimise the amount kept at the workplace;
- dispense and use in a safe place with adequate natural or mechanical ventilation;
- keep containers closed, eg use safety containers with self-closing lids and caps;
- contain spillages, eg by dispensing over a tray and having absorbent material handy;
- control ignition sources, eg naked flames and sparks, and make sure that 'no smoking' rules are obeyed, especially when spraying highly flammable liquids;
- keep contaminated material in a lidded metal bin which is emptied regularly;
- get rid of waste safely, eg burn rubbish in a suitable container well away from buildings;
- have fire extinguishers on hand. Don't burn aerosol cans and don't 'brighten' fires with flammable liquids.

HSE Infoline 0845 345 0055 HSE website www.hse.gov.uk HSE Books 01787 881165

Gas cylinders

Storage and use

■ Store both full and empty cylinders in a secure outside compound where possible.

■ Store with valves uppermost, particularly where they contain liquid like acetylene.

■ Don't store cylinders below ground level or near to drains or basements – most gases are heavier than air.

■ Protect cylinders from damage, eg by chaining unstable cylinders in racks or on special trolleys.

■ Use the right hoses, clamps, couplers and regulators for the particular gas and appliance.

■ Turn off cylinder valves at the end of each day's work.

■ Change cylinders away from sources of ignition, in a well-ventilated place.

■ Avoid welding flame 'flash-back' into the hoses or cylinders by training operators in correct lighting-up and working procedures and by fitting non-return valves and flame arresters.

■ Use soap or detergent/water solution, never a flame, to test for leaks.

■ Before welding and similar work, remove or protect flammable material.

■ Where possible, position gas cylinders on the outside of buildings and pipe through to appliances or processes.

■ Make sure that rooms where appliances, eg LPG heaters, are used have enough ventilation high up and low down, which is never blocked up to protect draughts.

Oxygen

Common materials may burn violently at high temperature in the presence of oxygen.

■ Never use oxygen to 'sweeten' the atmosphere.

■ Make sure there are no leaks, especially in confined areas, and don't use oxygen to operate compressed-air equipment.

■ Keep oxygen cylinders free from grease and other combustible materials and don't store them with flammable gases or materials.

Dust explosions

Do you have a dusty process? Is the dust flammable? Examples include aluminium powder, flour, bone-meal, cotton fly, paper dust, polystyrene and fine sawdust.

If so you must:

■ keep plant dust-tight and frequently checked and cleaned;

■ avoid build-up of dust, eg reduce the number of ledges and horizontal surfaces on which dust may settle and use exhaust ventilation with suitable dust collectors as necessary;

■ control sources of heat such as welding, space heaters and smoking;

■ reduce sparking by using dust-tight electrical equipment, by earthing sources of static electricity, and by using magnets to catch any stray pieces of metal before they get into the process;

■ take explosion-protection measures, by providing explosion vents or a plant structure strong enough to withstand an explosion;

■ make sure explosion vents discharge safely.

You can reduce the effects of an explosion by using lightweight construction for buildings which house dangerous plant.

Flammable solids

■ Plastic foams are high fire risk and need careful control, both for storage and in the workroom – treat them like other flammable materials.

■ Use non-sparking tools when scraping deposits from spray booths etc.

If you are a supplier

You must:

- provide safety data sheets and other information for users;
- if supplying a new substance see the 'Special cases' section;
- arrange for any necessary testing and research so that substances can be used safely at work;
- choose packaging which provides protection for users and during conveyance and transport;
- provide labels which give adequate information about the risks and necessary precautions;
- remember you need to look at the Chemicals (Hazard Information and Packaging for Supply) Regulations 2002 (as amended) and the Carriage Regulations 2004.

Special cases

You must notify HSE:

- if you use or store certain listed 'major hazard' dangerous substances. You will have to demonstrate to your inspector that your are operating safely;
- if you market more than one tonne per year of a new substance.

The discharge of effluent, disposal and transport of waste, and the emission of smoke and chemicals to the atmosphere may need special precautions or authorisation. Contact your inspector or local authority for advice.

Transporting materials

If you transport and deliver materials off site, then you must:

- ensure the packages are suitable and correctly labelled as required for carriage by road, rail or sea transport;
- ensure the vehicle is suitable for the purpose;
- provide appropriate firefighting equipment;
- fit hazard panels/plates on delivery vehicles as required;
- check compatibility of loads;
- provide written information for the driver;
- train vehicle drivers on their duties, the hazards and risks involved and the necessary emergency procedures as required by the Carriage Regulations 2004.

Emergencies

Consider what could go wrong

- Could staff accidentally mix incompatible chemicals, eg bleach with other cleaners?
- Are you prepared for a large leak or spillage?
- What about hazardous by-products? Could mixing of waste chemicals in the drains cause a hazardous reaction or pollution?
- Are any special first-aid facilities or equipment required?
- Could emergency water supplies freeze up in winter?

More information is given on accidents and emergencies in Chapter 25. General fire precautions are covered in Chapter 4.

Find out more

Dangerous Substances and Explosive Atmospheres. Dangerous Substances and Explosive Atmospheres Regulations 2002. Approved Code of Practice and guidance L138 ISBN 0 7176 2203 7 (Also see L134, L135, L136 and L137 for more detailed information – contact HSE Books for details)

Approved supply list (eighth edition). Information approved for the classification and labelling of substances and preparations dangerous for supply. Chemicals (Hazard Information and Packaging for Supply) Regulations 2002 (as amended) L142 ISBN 0 7176 6138 5

Dispensing petrol: Assessing and controlling the risk of fire and explosion at sites where petrol is stored and dispensed as a fuel HSG146 ISBN 0 7176 1048 9

Safe working with flammable substances Leaflet INDG227

Safe use of petrol in garages Leaflet INDG331

Fire and explosion: How safe is your workplace? A short guide to the Dangerous Substances and Explosive Atmospheres Regulations Leaflet INDG370

For more information on the Carriage Regulations 2004, visit www.hse.gov.uk/cdg/manual/index.htm

19

Managing health

The hazards

More people die from work-related diseases than from workplace accidents. This chapter deals with health risks in general, stress, drugs and alcohol, and smoking.

The two biggest causes nationally of work-related ill health are pain due to back problems, upper limb damage or 'dodgy knees' (see Chapter 12) and stress.

Also see Chapter 16 for radiation risks and Chapter 17 for information on health risks from harmful substances. Emergency arrangements and first aid are covered in Chapter 25.

Managing sickness absence and return to work

Sickness absence can have a big impact on the performance of your business and the health and well-being of your employees. Most is short-term but it can turn into long-term absence if action is not taken early enough to support their return to work.

By putting in place a policy to manage sickness absence and return to work you can minimise the effects on both your business and your workers.

- Regular recording of sickness absence will enable you to keep up to date with who is off sick and why. This will also tell you about trends in your workplace and where there are particular hotspots that may need your intervention.
- Keep in contact with those who are off sick to let them know what is happening at work and plan cover for their absence. This needs to be handled sensitively as some people may see this as a way to press them to return to work.
- Plan and carry out workplace adjustments to return your employee to their existing job or to an alternative if possible, to retain valuable skills and to remove barriers that would make return to work difficult. Take professional advice if discussions with your employee do not provide solutions. Your employee's GP may be able to help but do not contact them without your employee's consent.

The law

Under the Health and Safety at Work etc Act 1974 (the HSW Act), you have a legal duty to ensure, so far as is reasonably practicable, the health, safety and welfare at work of your employees.

The Management of Health and Safety at Work Regulations 1999 (the Management Regulations) require you to assess and control risks to protect your employees.

- If your employee is or becomes disabled, the law requires you to make reasonable adjustments to enable them to continue working. You may need to seek professional advice where appropriate.
- A return-to-work interview is enough for most employees to discuss any concerns they may have. However, for those in danger of becoming long-term sick, a return-to-work plan is important. These plans should be kept under close review.
- Appoint someone to co-ordinate the return-to-work process to make sure the plan proceeds smoothly and everyone involved knows what is expected. Whoever is chosen should be familiar with the employee's work, be able to negotiate at all levels and be sensitive to the needs of the employee.

How to make it happen

- You and your senior managers need to be committed to implementing and supporting a policy for managing sickness absence and return to work.
- Your line managers need the skills and confidence to manage sickness absence and return to work.
- You, your line managers, your employees and their representatives need to work together to ensure sickness absence is tackled fairly and consistently.

If you need help

- Contact HSE's Infoline (Tel: 0845 345 0055) or visit www.hse.gov.uk/sicknessabsence.
- Contact local occupational health support services or Workplace Health Connect (Tel: 0845 609 6066).
- For expert advice there are a number of occupational health providers including NHS Plus. Other sources of advice include rehabilitation providers, specialists in rehabilitation medicine, case managers, disability and rehabilitation charities, insurers and Jobcentre Plus.

Find out more

Managing sickness absence and return to work in small businesses Leaflet INDG399

Managing sickness absence and return to work: An employers' and managers' guide HSG249 ISBN 0 7176 2882 5

Workplace Health Connect website: www.hse.gov.uk/workplacehealth/index.htm

Health surveillance

Health surveillance means having a system to look for early signs of ill health caused by substances and other hazards at work. It includes keeping health records for individuals and may include medical examinations and testing of blood or urine samples, so that corrective action can be taken.

Health surveillance is not required for most workers. You must decide whether it is needed for what you do. If in doubt, eg if there are known health risks from the work, get advice.

Medical examinations or health surveillance are required by law for some jobs. Ask yourself whether any of your employees is at risk from:

- noise or vibration (see Chapters 13 and 14);
- solvents, fumes, dusts, biological agents and other substances hazardous to health (see Chapter 17);
- asbestos, lead or work in compressed air (see Chapter 17);
- ionising radiations (see Chapter 16) or commercial diving.

Special conditions apply to some people who are particularly at risk, such as pregnant women whose jobs may expose them to lead or ionising radiations (see Chapter 23).

Involve your employees and their representatives at an early stage, so they understand their roles and responsibilities in any health surveillance programme.

Ask for advice from a competent person if you need to, such as an occupational health professional.

Find out more

Health surveillance at work HSG61 (Second edition) ISBN 0 7176 1705 X

Understanding health surveillance at work: An introduction for employers Leaflet INDG304

Work-related stress

The risks

Pressure is part of all work and helps to keep us motivated and productive. But excessive pressure can lead to stress, which undermines performance, is costly to employers, and can make people ill.

What you must do

As an employer, under the HSW Act you have a 'duty of care' to protect the health, safety and welfare of all employees while at work. You also have to assess the risks arising from hazards at work, including work-related stress, in accordance with the Management Regulations.

An effective risk assessment approach to tackling stress should include the following:

■ Measure the current situation (using surveys and/or other techniques).
■ Have discussions with employees and their representatives.
■ Work in partnership with employees and their representatives to make practical improvements.
■ Agree and share an action plan with employees and their representatives.
■ Regularly review the situation to ensure it continues to improve.

Management Standards for Work-related Stress

HSE's Management Standards for Work-related Stress cover six key areas of work that, if not properly managed, are associated with poor health and well-being, lower productivity, and increased sickness absence. These are:

■ Demands – workload, work patterns and the work environment.
■ Control – how much say the person has in the way they do their work.
■ Support – the encouragement and support provided by the organisation, managers and colleagues.
■ Relationships – working to avoid conflict and dealing with unacceptable behaviour.
■ Role – whether people understand their role within the organisation and whether the organisation ensures they do not have conflicting roles.
■ Change – how change is managed and communicated in the organisation.

The Management Standards approach provides a framework and process against which to develop an effective risk assessment, and is supported by a toolkit designed to help organisations measure and improve their performance in tackling stress.

Is stress a problem in your workplace?

There are a number of ways to identify the causes of stress in your workplace:

■ Use existing information to see how your organisation shapes up. Sickness absence or staff turnover data could help, as well as employee surveys.
■ Conduct a stress survey of employees to find out potential problem areas as part of an overall strategy to identify and address the sources of stress. (See www.hse.gov.uk/stress/standards for free Stress Indicator and Analysis Tools.)
■ Have discussions with employees to assess what causes stress in your workplace and identify relevant problems and solutions.

Develop solutions

■ Continue to talk to employees to identify issues that affect them at work and discuss practical solutions.
■ Record what you decide to do in an action plan, share it with staff and stick to it.
■ Include a review of your risk assessment in your action plan, to check how effective your actions are.

Find out more

Real solutions, real people: A managers' guide to tackling work-related stress ISBN 0 7176 2767 5

Tackling stress: The Management Standards approach Leaflet INDG406

Working together to reduce stress at work: A guide for employees Leaflet MISC686

Making the Stress Management Standards work: How to apply the Standards in your workplace Leaflet MISC714

Stress Management Standards web pages: www.hse.gov.uk/stress/standards

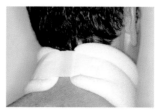

Second-hand smoking

Scotland

From 26 March 2006 smoking in Scotland has been banned under public health legislation in almost all workplaces. This includes vehicles used for business purposes and public transport.

Exemptions include residential accommodation, designated rooms in adult care homes, adult hospices, psychiatric hospitals and units, and offshore installations. Designated detention or interview rooms and private vehicles are also exempted. Employers in exempted premises are still required to reduce the risk to their employees from second-hand smoking to as low a level as is reasonably practicable.

England and Wales

From summer 2007, a smoking ban will be introduced in England with a limited number of exemptions along the lines of Scotland. The Welsh Assembly Government has also indicated that it will be introducing a comprehensive ban. Until then, employers should continue to protect employees from the effects of second-hand smoke and:

- have a specific policy on smoking in the workplace;
- take action to reduce the risk to the health and safety of their employees from second-hand smoke to as low a level as is reasonably practicable;
- make sure their smoking policy gives priority to the needs of non-smokers who do not wish to breathe tobacco smoke;
- consult employees and their representatives on the appropriate smoking policy to suit their workplace.

Find out more

Scotland
For more information visit: www.clearingtheairscotland.com

The *Smoke-free Scotland* guidance contains advice for the NHS, local authorities and care service providers: www.scotland.gov.uk/Resource/doc/47121/0020880.pdf

England and Wales
For more information contact the Department of Health Customer Service Centre on 020 7210 4850 or visit: www.dh.gov.uk/PolicyAndGuidance/HealthAndSocialCare Topics/Tobacco/fs/en

Drugs and alcohol

- Abuse of alcohol, drugs and other substances can affect health, work performance and safety.
- Learn to recognise the signs and encourage workers to seek help.
- Be supportive.
- If you decide strict standards are needed because of safety-critical jobs, then agree procedures with your workers in advance. Disciplinary action may be needed where safety is critical.

Violence at work

People who deal directly with the public may face aggressive or violent behaviour. They may be sworn at, threatened or even attacked. Physical attacks are obviously dangerous but serious or persistent verbal abuse or threats can also damage employees' health through anxiety or stress.

What to do

- Ask your employees whether they ever feel threatened and encourage them to report incidents.
- Keep detailed records, including of verbal abuse and threats.
- Try to predict what might happen – there may be a known pattern of violence linked to certain work situations.
- Train your employees so that they can spot the early signs of aggression and avoid it or cope with it.
- Consider physical security measures, eg video cameras or alarm systems and coded security locks on doors.
- Support victims, eg with debriefing or specialist counselling and time off work to recover.

Find out more

Work-related violence: Case studies – Managing the risk in smaller businesses HSG229 ISBN 0 7176 2358 0

Violence at work: A guide for employers Leaflet INDG69

Drug misuse at work: A guide for employers Leaflet INDG91(rev2)

Don't mix it: A guide for employers on alcohol at work Leaflet INDG240

20

Safe ways of working

The hazards

Everyone makes mistakes or takes short-cuts from time to time, so it is important to try and make the workplace safe even if this happens, eg by guarding machinery so people cannot reach the dangerous parts.

Making the workplace safe includes providing instructions, procedures, training and supervision to encourage people to work safely and responsibly.

That is also why there are 'permit-to-work' systems for non-routine or higher-hazard work.

Involving your workers in managing health and safety is important. Often they have good ideas about how to work more safely and their involvement helps them to more readily accept any precautions.

Safe systems and procedures

- Make sure employees are well-trained or skilled and understand the hazards and risks of the work they have to do.
- Make sure there are safe systems and procedures for routine work (including setting up and preparation, finishing off and cleaning activities).
- Make sure there are written procedures for work that is done less often or is high risk, eg maintenance, repairs or unusual jobs.
- Make sure you consider issues such as workload or job design if you want the procedures to be followed properly.
- Don't forget to consider emergencies, eg fire, spillages or plant breakdown (see Chapter 25).
- Supervise to make sure people are actually following the safe systems and procedures, especially for work which is high risk or where vulnerable people are involved.
- Take action when instructions, rules or procedures are not being followed.

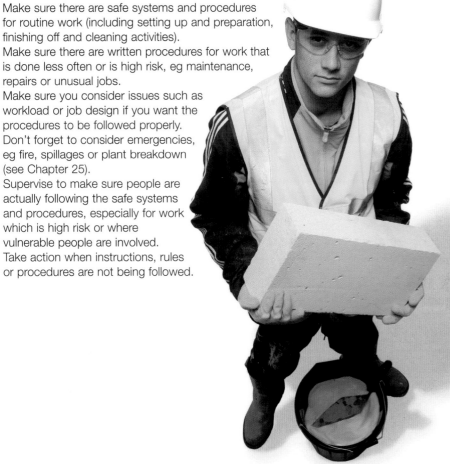

The law

Section 2 of the Health and Safety at Work etc Act 1974 (the HSW Act) requires 'safe systems of work', but does not go into detail. This chapter gives advice on what this means in practice.

Look at the Management of Health and Safety at Work Regulations 1999 for the requirement to make appropriate arrangements for managing health and safety.

For information on involving employees in decisions about health and safety in the workplace, look at the Health and Safety (Consultation with Employees) Regulations 1996 and the Safety Representatives and Safety Committees Regulations 1977.

Points to consider

- Are safe ways of doing the job already understood and being carried out?
- Is the job complex, risky or so infrequently done that a written step-by-step procedure, checklist, or diagram might help?
- If so, are the procedures designed and written simply and clearly, with information on any key hazards?
- Is it clear who is in charge of the job?
- Is it clear who does what, with no important gaps or overlaps?
- Has anyone checked that the equipment, tools or machines are appropriate (and available) for the job?
- Could this job harm others, eg people working nearby, or the public and how will they be protected?
- If the job cannot be finished today will it be left in a safe state and are clear instructions available for the next shift?
- Are other people aware of what maintenance staff are doing and vice versa?
- Do people know what might go wrong, eg accident, explosion, food poisoning, electrocution, fire, release of radioactivity, chemical spill and what to do if these happen?
- Plan to review your procedures from time to time, to make sure they are still relevant and do not need improving.

Involve employees

Employers have to consult their employees or their representatives on health and safety issues. This is important because:

- employees know exactly what goes on in the workplace, so they have knowledge that managers might not have about working practices and risks, and can help develop practical solutions to problems;
- if employees feel they are actively involved in making decisions about health and safety, they are much more likely to co-operate with their employers and come forward with new ideas.

Practical ways to involve employees

- Involve employees in risk assessments or investigations.
- Carry out surveys of particular workplaces, activities or hazards, followed up by discussions with employees to create an action plan.
- Find solutions to specific health and safety problems through a team of employees or a workshop. Make it clear what they are expected to do, and by when.
- Hold briefing sessions on changes at work. Team discussions or 'toolbox talks' are useful to let people know what is happening and also to receive feedback.
- Use suggestion boxes to help people who are shy about talking in public have their say. But make sure you respond to the suggestions.

Appointed representatives

In organisations that recognise a trade union, the union is entitled to appoint 'safety representatives'. They have a number of legal rights, including the right to some paid time off to make investigations or inspections of the workplace, and to be trained to carry out their duties. You can consult the workforce through them at safety committees or other joint committees, and you can get them to help you with wider involvement of employees.

If your organisation does not recognise trade unions, you still must consult employees on health and safety matters. You can do this either by contacting all employees directly, or by electing 'representatives of employee safety'. They have many of the same rights and functions as trade union safety representatives.

Permits to work

Simple instructions or procedures are adequate for most jobs, but some require extra care. A 'permit to work' states exactly what work is to be done and when, and which parts are safe. A responsible person should assess the work and check safety at each stage. The people doing the job sign the permit to show that they understand the risks and precautions necessary.

Examples of high-risk jobs where a written 'permit-to-work' procedure may need to be used include:

- entry into vessels, confined spaces or machines;
- hot work (welding, grinding or flame cutting) which could cause a fire or explosion;
- construction work or the use of contractors;

- cutting into pipework carrying hazardous substances;
- mechanical or electrical work requiring isolation of the power source, eg before work inside large machines, if locking off is not good enough;
- work on plant, mixers, boilers etc which must be effectively cut off from the possible entry of fumes, gas liquids or steam;
- testing for dangerous fumes or lack of oxygen before entering an unventilated pit or silo;
- vacuuming the inside of an empty grain silo to remove dust which might explode, before hot cutting a hole in the side.

When the risk is high, precautions should be 100% correct. If in doubt get competent advice, eg from the company who gives you Employers' Liability Insurance, or from a trade body.

Lock-off procedures

Before working on plant or equipment, isolate machines from all power sources securely, eg isolate them from the main power supply by locking off the main electrical supply switch.

■ Use a safety lock with one key.
■ Where several people are working, use a multiple hasp so that everyone can fit their own lock.
■ Only when all the locks have been removed can the equipment be switched on.
■ Put a clear warning notice or label on the switch, and make sure it is removed when the work has finished.

Supervise

Employers, managers and supervisors must check that employees are working safely, and take effective action when they are not.

■ Don't ignore unsafe or unhealthy working and always deal with it immediately.
■ People usually believe that they have a good reason for working as they do, so find out why and tackle the underlying reasons.
■ Be prepared to use disciplinary action as a last resort for repeated or very serious cases.

Find out more

Management of health and safety at work. Management of Health and Safety at Work Regulations 1999. Approved Code of Practice and guidance L21 (Second edition) ISBN 0 7176 2488 9

Safety representatives and safety committees L87 (Third edition) ISBN 0 7176 1220 1

A guide to the Health and Safety (Consultation with Employees) Regulations 1996. Guidance on Regulations L95 ISBN 0 7176 1234 1

Reducing error and influencing behaviour HSG48 (Second edition) ISBN 0 7176 2452 8

Guidance on permit-to-work systems: A guide for the petroleum, chemical and allied industries HSG250 ISBN 0 7176 2943 0

The safe isolation of plant and equipment HSG253 ISBN 0 7176 6171 7

Consulting employees on health and safety: A guide to the law Leaflet INDG232

Visit www.hse.gov.uk/workers for more information on worker involvement.

Selection and training

The hazards

People are a danger to themselves or others if they cannot do their jobs correctly, or if their ways of working, where this matters for health and safety, are not clearly agreed, set out and checked.

This can be because they are in jobs for which they are unsuited and/or are not competent, or for which the procedures are inadequate, unrealistic or unchecked (see Chapter 20). It could also be because their training is not linked adequately to relevant risk assessments and key procedures.

Selection

- Identify jobs which place particular physical or mental demands on people – can these be changed to cut out or reduce the demands?
- Where you cannot do this you need to select people to meet the demands.
- Identify the essential health and safety requirements of a job and use them during recruitment, eg colour-blindness checks for people being recruited to work on wiring or control panels.
- For some jobs, eg driving heavy goods vehicles, the law requires medical examinations, but pre-employment medical checks are not legally required for most jobs.
- People returning after illness may need help readjusting to their jobs – seek specialist medical advice if necessary (see Chapter 19).

The law

The Management of Health and Safety at Work Regulations 1999 set down some general requirements.

Some groups, such as young people, new and expectant mothers and those with a disability, need special consideration (see Chapter 23).

HSE Infoline 0845 345 0055 **HSE website** www.hse.gov.uk **HSE Books** 01787 881165

Training

■ You must ensure all employees (as well as their managers and supervisors) are trained in the significant health and safety hazards and risks of their work and workplace and how to avoid them.
■ Making people competent needs more than just formal training – they also need a well-structured introduction to the actual work ('on-the-job' training) including familiarisation with the main procedures, time to practise what they have learnt, and suitable assessment where this is important.

Also think about:

■ any legal requirements for specific job training, eg lift trucks, first aid;
■ the special needs of young people, new recruits, trainees and part-time employees;
■ appropriate refresher training for existing workers, especially when changes are made in the workplace, and targeted training for those moving jobs;
■ training needs identified during investigations, risk assessments or from checks/audits;
■ whether to give the training yourself or to get some outside help;
■ setting suitable and clear site- and job-specific performance standards for key roles, jobs and work. There may be existing standards of competence for what you do, eg NVQs or SVQs.

Find out more

Effective health and safety training: A trainer's resource pack HSG222 ISBN 0 7176 2109 X

Health and safety training: What you need to know Leaflet INDG345

HSE Infoline 0845 345 0055 **HSE website** www.hse.gov.uk **HSE Books** 01787 881165

21 Selection and training

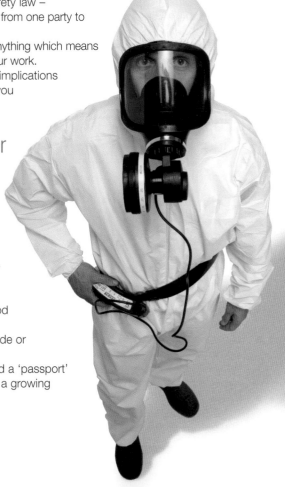

Contractors and agency workers

The hazards

Contractors are often used for particularly hazardous jobs, so it is essential that you work with them to make sure the job is carried out properly while protecting workers and anyone else (eg visitors or members of the public).

Agency workers may be at increased risk of work-related illness and injury compared to permanent employees, because they are unfamiliar with the business and its hazards.

Employing contractors

■ If you employ contractors, both you and the contractor will have duties under health and safety law – responsibilities cannot be passed on from one party to another by a contract.

■ Make sure you do not contract out anything which means you lose control of critical areas of your work.

■ Think through the health and safety implications of the job, and what arrangements you need to make.

Select a suitable contractor

Make sure you take on a contractor who is competent to do the job safely and find out:

■ whether they have relevant experience, qualifications and skills in the type of work you want done – ask for references;

■ how they select subcontractors;

■ whether they provide a safety method statement (for building work);

■ if they are members of a relevant trade or professional body;

■ whether they or their employees hold a 'passport' in health and safety training – this is a growing trend in some industries.

The law

The Health and Safety at Work etc Act 1974 (the HSW Act) places duties on employers and contractors to protect the health and safety of employees and other people who may be affected by their work activities. It also deals with information, instruction and training.

The Management of Health and Safety at Work Regulations 1999 require all employers who share a workplace to co-operate and co-ordinate their work to ensure everyone is complying with their legal duties, and to keep workers from other undertakings working on their site informed about risks and measures to protect their health and safety.

The Construction (Design and Management) Regulations 1994 place specific legal responsibilities on clients, contractors and others (see Chapter 6).

Assess the risks of the work

- Agree beforehand exactly what is to be done, by whom and how.
- Agree with the contractor the risk assessment for the job and the procedures for safe working that will apply when the work is in progress.
- If subcontractors are involved, they should also be part of the discussion and agreement.

Provide information, instruction and training

- Make sure the contractor's employees understand your rules for safe working, as well as any hazards and precautions, and that you understand theirs.
- Each new employee coming on site should receive appropriate instruction and training and be made aware of the hazards in your workplace and any emergency procedures.

Manage and supervise

- Liaise with contractors, check their health and safety performance on site and make sure you keep each other informed about hazards and changes to plans or systems of work which may affect health and safety.
- Where health and safety requirements are not being met, you and the contractor need to find out why and sort out the problem.

Find out more

Managing contractors: A guide for employers. An open learning booklet HSG159 ISBN 0 7176 1196 5

Working together: Guidance on health and safety for contractors and suppliers
www.hse.gov.uk/pubns/indg268.pdf (web only)

Use of contractors: A joint responsibility Leaflet INDG368

Agency workers

Employment agencies and employment businesses have specific legal responsibilities under the Conduct of Employment Agencies and Employment Businesses Regulations 2003 to provide information to businesses who use their workers.

Both employment businesses and hirers need to do the following to protect agency workers:

- Make sure, before they start work, that they are included in risk assessments, and that they know what measures have been taken as a result to protect them.
- Make sure they understand the information and instructions they need to work safely, and that they have had any necessary training.
- Remember to consider any language needs there may be for agency workers who do not speak English well or at all (see Chapter 23).
- Check, before they start at the workplace, that they have any special occupational qualifications or skills needed for the job.
- Agree on arrangements for providing any necessary health surveillance or computer screen eyesight tests, and for providing/maintaining any personal protective equipment needed.
- Agree on arrangements for reporting relevant accidents to the enforcing authority.

Find out more

Guidance on the Employment Agencies and Employment Businesses Regulations 2003
View online: www.dti.gov.uk/er/agency/conduct.pdf

For more guidance on managing the health and safety of agency workers visit:
www.businesslink.gov.uk/agencyworkers

23

Special groups of workers

The hazards

There are several groups of workers who need special consideration, so you need to think carefully how best to look after their needs and the needs of your business, for example young people, people with disabilities, workers for whom English is not their first language, new and expectant mothers and lone and mobile workers.

Young people

Young people, especially those new to the workplace, will face unfamiliar risks from the job they will be doing and from the working environment. In health and safety law:

- a young person is anyone under the age of eighteen;
- a child is anyone who has not reached the official age at which they may leave school.

Your responsibilities

You have particular responsibilities to assess the risks to all young people under 18 **before** they start work. Ensure your risk assessment takes into account:

- their immaturity, inexperience and lack of awareness of existing or potential risks;
- the fitting out and layout of the workplace and where they will work;
- the nature of any physical, biological and chemical agents they will be exposed to, for how long and how much;
- what equipment will be used and how it will be handled;
- how the work and processes are organised;
- the need to assess and provide health and safety training; and
- risks from particular agents and processes.

You need to introduce control measures to eliminate or minimise the risks, so far as reasonably practicable.

The law

The Management of Health and Safety at Work Regulations 1999 require employers to provide understandable information and instructions about risks and measures to protect health and safety. Section 2 of the Health and Safety at Work etc Act 1974 (the HSW Act) also deals with information, instruction and training.

The Employment of Women, Young Persons and Children Act 1920 prohibits the employment of school age children in industrial undertakings such as factories or construction sites, except when on approved work experience programmes. The Children and Young Persons Act 1933 allows local authorities to make byelaws to authorise the employment of children for certain types of light work.

If you employ disabled people you also have duties under the Disability Discrimination Act 1995.

You must also let the parents/guardians of any children still of compulsory school age know the key findings of the risk assessment and the control measures you have introduced **before** the child starts work or work experience.

Restrictions on the work of young people

You should not employ young people to do work which:

- is beyond their physical or psychological capacity;
- exposes them to radiation, or harmful substances, eg toxic or carcinogenic;
- involves a risk of accidents that they are unlikely to recognise because of lack of experience or training;
- involves a risk to their health from extreme heat, noise or vibration.

Training and supervision

- Ensure they receive appropriate training **and check they understand the key messages**.
- Provide training and instruction on the hazards and risks in the workplace and on the measures to protect their health and safety.
- Include a basic introduction to first-aid, fire and evacuation procedures.
- Ensure young people are supervised. This will help monitor the effectiveness of the training they receive, and help to assess whether they have the necessary capacity and competence to do the job.

Work experience

When you offer someone a work experience placement it is important to recognise that you have the same responsibilities for their health, safety and welfare as for the rest of the workforce and they will be regarded as being your employee.

Find out more

Young people at work: A guide for employers HSG165 (Second edition) ISBN 0 7176 1889 7

Managing health and safety on work experience: A guide for organisers HSG199 ISBN 0 7176 1742 4

The right start: Work experience for young people – Health and safety basics for employers Leaflet INDG364

People with disabilities

You have a duty under health and safety law to ensure the health, safety and welfare of all employees, whether or not they are disabled.

You also have duties under the Disability Discrimination Act 1995 to make reasonable adjustments to accommodate employees who are or have become disabled, as defined by the Act.

- When you think that a person's disability may affect health and safety, it is sensible to have a new risk assessment carried out by a suitably qualified person.
- The fact that a person has a disability does not mean they represent an additional risk to health and safety.
- In most cases, health and safety responsibilities should not be a barrier to continuing to employ or recruit disabled people.

Find out more

Managing sickness absence and return to work: An employers' and managers' guide HSG249 ISBN 0 7176 2882 5 (includes information on how to plan and carry out workplace adjustments)

Disability Discrimination Act 1995 Code of Practice – Employment and Occupation View online on the Disability Rights Commission website: www.drc-gb.org/index.asp

Language provision

If your workforce includes people who do not speak or understand English well or at all, they may be at greater risk because of this, so you must make sure they get health and safety information, instruction and training they can understand.

Understandable information, instruction and training

How much you need to do will depend partly on the level of risk they face. You could:

- use a work colleague who already has a good understanding of the information to interpret it into the worker's language;
- get information translated by a speaker of the workers' language who also speaks good English and can best judge how to explain it clearly;
- use audio tapes or videos if workers cannot read, or speak a language which has no written form;
- use internationally-understood pictorial signs where possible;
- if training courses are run in English, use simpler training materials, including visuals where possible and time for questions;
- consider English-language courses for longer-term workers;
- ensure newly-trained workers are supervised. To begin with, pair a newly-trained non-English speaker with a more experienced worker who speaks the same language;
- monitor workers to see how much they have understood and take action to re-train or provide instruction and information in a different way, if there is still a need.

Find out more

Your health, your safety is available online in many languages: www.hse.gov.uk/languages/index.htm

New and expectant mothers

You are required to conduct a risk assessment for all employees which should include any specific risks to females of child-bearing age. You are also required to take into account risks to new and expectant mothers.

Some of the more common risks might be:

- lifting or carrying heavy loads;
- standing or sitting for long periods;
- exposure to infectious diseases;
- exposure to lead;
- work-related stress;
- workstations and posture;
- exposure to radioactive material;
- other people's smoke in the workplace;
- long working hours.

When an employee notifies you in writing that she is pregnant, you should carry out a specific risk assessment based on the outcome of your initial risk assessment. This also applies if she has given birth in the previous six months or is breastfeeding. If there is a significant risk to the health and safety of a new or expectant mother, you must take the following actions to remove her from the risk:

- temporarily adjust the person's working conditions and hours of work;
- offer suitable alternative work;
- suspend her from work on paid leave to protect her health and safety or that of her child.

Find out more

New and expectant mothers at work: A guide for employers HSG122 (Second edition) ISBN 0 7176 2583 4

A guide for new and expectant mothers who work Leaflet INDG373

New and expectant mothers at work: A guide for health professionals www.hse.gov.uk/pubns/indg373hp.pdf (web only)

Lone and mobile workers

Lone workers who work without close or direct supervision and mobile workers who work away from their fixed base need special consideration.

When your risk assessment shows that it is not possible for the work to be done safely by a lone worker, provide help or back-up.

Consider:

- What are the foreseeable emergencies, eg fire, equipment failure, illness and accidents?
- Does the workplace present a special risk to the lone worker?
- Can all the plant, equipment, substances and goods involved in the work be safely handled by one person?
- Does the work involve lifting objects or operating controls that really require more than one person?
- Is there a risk of violence?
- Are women or young workers especially at risk if they work alone?
- What training is required?
- Is the person medically fit and suitable to work alone?

Monitor lone workers, for example:

- Make sure there is regular contact with the lone worker using visits, telephone or radio.
- Provide automatic warning devices to raise the alarm if there is an emergency.
- Check that a lone worker has returned to base after completing a job.

Find out more

Working alone in safety: Controlling the risks of solitary work Leaflet INDG73(rev)

HSE Infoline 0845 345 0055   **HSE website** www.hse.gov.uk   **HSE Books** 01787 881165

23 Special groups of workers

Personal protective equipment

The hazards

Even where engineering controls and safe systems of work have been applied, some hazards might remain. These include injuries to:

- the lungs, eg from breathing in contaminated air;
- the head and feet, eg from falling materials;
- the eyes, eg from flying particles or splashes of corrosive liquids;
- the skin, eg from contact with corrosive materials;
- the body, eg from extremes of heat or cold.

Personal protective equipment (PPE) is needed in these cases to reduce the risk.

The last resort

Use personal protective equipment (PPE) only as a last resort – wherever possible use engineering controls and safe systems of work instead. If PPE is still needed it must be provided free by the employer.

Selection and use

You must consider:

- who is exposed and to what?
- how long are they exposed for?
- how much are they exposed to?

You must:

- choose good quality products which are CE marked in accordance with the Personal Protective Equipment Regulations 2002 – suppliers can advise you;
- choose equipment which suits the wearer – consider the size, fit and weight. If you let the users help choose it, they will be more likely to use it;
- make sure it fits properly, eg it is difficult to create a good seal if a respirator user has a beard. For tight-fitting facepieces (filtering facepieces, half and full masks) a good seal can only be achieved if the wearer is clean shaven in the region of the seal;
- make sure that if more than one item of PPE is being worn they can be used together, eg a respirator may not give proper protection if air leaks in around the seal because the user is wearing safety glasses;
- instruct and train people how to use it. Tell them why it is needed, when to use it and what its limitations are.

Remember that PPE is a last resort but must be worn when needed.

The law

The Personal Protective Equipment Regulations 2002 and the Personal Protective Equipment at Work Regulations 1992 (as amended) give the main requirements, but other special regulations cover lead, asbestos, hazardous substances (see Chapter 17), noise (see Chapter 13) and radiation (see Chapter 16).

See also the Construction (Head Protection) Regulations 1989.

Other advice

- Many solvents quickly go through rubber-based materials. Few materials protect you if soaked in hazardous chemicals.
- Never allow exemptions for those jobs which take 'just a few minutes'.
- Check with your supplier – explain the job to them.
- If in doubt seek further advice from your inspector or other specialist adviser.

Maintenance

Equipment must be properly looked after and stored when not in use, eg in a dry, clean cupboard. If it is reusable it must be cleaned and kept in good condition.

Think about:

- using the right replacement parts which match the original, eg respirator filters;
- keeping replacement PPE available;
- who is responsible for maintenance and how it is to be done;
- having a supply of appropriate disposable suits which are useful for dirty jobs where laundry costs are high, eg for visitors who need protective clothing.

Employees must make proper use of PPE and report its loss or destruction or any fault in it.

Monitor and review

- Check regularly that PPE is used or find out why not. Safety signs can be a useful reminder.
- Take note of any changes in equipment, materials and methods – you may need to update what you provide.

Eyes

Hazards
Chemical or metal splash, dust, projectiles, gas and vapour, radiation.

Options
Safety spectacles, goggles, face screens, faceshields, visors.

Note
Make sure the eye protection chosen has the right combination of impact/dust/splash/molten metal eye protection for the task and fits the user properly.

Head and neck

Hazards
Impact from falling or flying objects, risk of head bumping, hair entanglement, chemical drips or splash, climate or temperature.

Options
Industrial safety helmets, bump caps, hairnets and firefighters' helmets.

Note
Some safety helmets incorporate or can be fitted with specially-designed eye or hearing protection. Don't forget neck protection, eg scarves for use during welding. Replace head protection if it is damaged.

Ears

Hazards
Impact noise, high intensities (even if short exposure), pitch (high and low frequency).

Options
Earplugs or earmuffs.

Note
Earplugs may fit into or cover the ear canal to form a seal. Earmuffs are normally hard plastic cups which fit over and surround the ears. They are sealed to the head by cushion seals. Take advice to make sure they reduce noise to an acceptable level. Fit only specially-designed earmuffs over safety helmets. See Chapter 13 for more information on noise.

Hands and arms

Hazards
Abrasion, temperature extremes, cuts and punctures, impact, chemicals, electric shock, skin irritation, disease or contamination.

Options
Gloves, gloves with a cuff, gauntlets and sleeving which covers part of or the whole of the arm.

Note
Don't wear gloves when operating machines such as bench drills where the gloves might get caught. Some materials are quickly penetrated by chemicals – take care in selection. Use skin-conditioning cream after work with water or fat solvents. Barrier creams are unreliable and are no substitute for proper PPE. Disposable or cotton inner gloves can reduce the effects of sweating.

Feet and legs

Hazards
Wet, hot and cold conditions, electrostatic build-up, slipping, cuts and punctures, falling objects, heavy loads, metal and chemical splash, vehicles.

Options
Safety boots and shoes with protective toe caps and penetration-resistant mid-sole, wellington boots and specific footwear, eg foundry boots and chainsaw boots.

Note
Footwear can have a variety of sole patterns and materials to help prevent slips in different conditions, can have oil or chemical-resistant soles, and can be anti-static, electrically conductive or thermally insulating. There is a variety of styles including 'trainers' and ankle supports. Avoid high-heeled shoes and open sandals. Consider the comfort factor for the wearer.

Lungs

Hazards
Oxygen-deficient atmospheres, dusts, gases and vapours.

Options
There are respirators that rely on filtering contaminants from workplace air. These include simple filtering facepieces and respirators and power-assisted respirators. In addition there are types of breathing apparatus, which give an independent supply of breathable air, for example fresh-air hose, compressed airline and self-contained breathing apparatus. You will need to use breathing apparatus in a confined space or if there is a chance of an oxygen deficiency in the work area.

Note
The right type of respirator filter must be used as each is effective for only a limited range of substances. Filters have only a limited life. Where there is a shortage of oxygen or any danger of losing consciousness due to exposure to high levels of harmful fumes, use only breathing apparatus – never use a filtering cartridge. If you are using respiratory protective equipment look at HSE's publication HSG53.

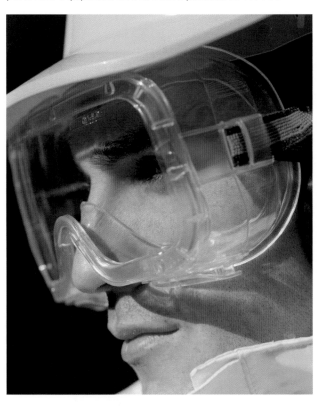

Whole body

Hazards

Heat, cold, bad weather, chemical or metal splash, spray from pressure leaks or spray guns, contaminated dust, impact or penetration, excessive wear or entanglement of own clothing.

Options

Conventional or disposable overalls, boiler suits, aprons, chemical suits, thermal clothing.

Note

The choice of materials includes flame retardant, anti-static, chain mail, chemically impermeable, and high visibility. Don't forget other protection, like safety harnesses or life jackets.

Emergency equipment

Careful selection, maintenance and regular and realistic operator training is needed for equipment like compressed-air escape breathing apparatus, respirators and safety ropes or harnesses.

Find out more

Personal protective equipment at work (Second edition).
Personal Protective Equipment at Work Regulations 1992.
Guidance on Regulations 1992 (as amended) L25
ISBN 0 7176 6139 3

Respiratory protective equipment at work: A practical guide HSG53 (Third edition) ISBN 0 7176 2904 X

A short guide to the Personal Protective Equipment at Work Regulations 1992 Leaflet INDG174(rev1)

Chainsaws at work Leaflet INDG317

Here is an example of a chainsaw user who has:

- A safety helmet – replace as recommended by the manufacturer, eg at least every 2 to 3 years.
- Ear defenders.
- Eye protection.
- Clothing – should be close fitting.
- Gloves – with protective pad on the back of the left hand.
- Protection for legs – incorporating loosely-woven long nylon fibres or similar material. All-round leg protection is recommended for occasional users.
- Chainsaw operator boots – where there is little risk of tripping or snagging the casual user may obtain adequate protection by a combination of protective spats and industrial steel toe-capped safety boots.

Accidents and emergencies

The hazards

In any business, things sometimes go wrong. You need to be ready to deal with these unplanned events and minimise the potential consequences.

Look at past incidents which have caused injuries and ill health or other damage to see what you can learn.

Think about emergencies and plan for the worst that can happen. You must have the right first-aid arrangements.

Some events need to be reported – this chapter tells you how to do this.

Fire precautions are covered in Chapter 4.

Emergency procedures

Special procedures are necessary for emergencies such as serious injuries, explosion, flood, poisoning, electrocution, fire, release of radioactivity and chemical spills. Quick and effective action by people may help to ease the situation and reduce the consequences.

However, in emergencies people are more likely to respond reliably if they are well trained and competent, take part in regular and realistic practice, and have clearly agreed, recorded and rehearsed plans, actions and responsibilities.

Write an emergency plan if a major incident at your workplace could involve risks to the public, rescuing employees or co-ordination of the emergency services.

The law

The Management of Health and Safety at Work Regulations 1999 cover emergencies. The requirements for first aid are in the Health and Safety (First Aid) Regulations 1981, and for reporting incidents in the Reporting of Injuries, Diseases and Dangerous Occurrences Regulations 1995 (RIDDOR).

The Dangerous Substances (Notification and Marking of Sites) Regulations 1990 cover sites where at least 25 tonnes of dangerous substances are held.

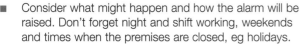

25 Accidents and emergencies

Points to include in emergency procedures

- Consider what might happen and how the alarm will be raised. Don't forget night and shift working, weekends and times when the premises are closed, eg holidays.
- Plan what to do, including how to call the emergency services. Help them by clearly marking your premises from the road. Consider drawing up a simple plan showing the location of hazardous items.
- If you have at least 25 tonnes of dangerous substances you must notify the fire and rescue authority and put up warning signs.
- Decide where to go to reach a place of safety or to get rescue equipment. Provide emergency lighting if necessary.
- You must make sure there are enough emergency exits for everyone to escape quickly, and keep emergency doors and escape routes unobstructed and clearly marked.
- Nominate competent persons to take control.
- Decide who are the other key people, such as a nominated incident controller, someone who is able to provide technical and other site-specific information if necessary, or first-aiders?
- Plan essential actions such as emergency plant shut-down, isolation or making processes safe. Clearly identify important items like shut-off valves and electrical isolators etc.
- You must train everyone in emergency procedures. Don't forget the needs of people with disabilities.

Reporting injuries and other events

RIDDOR applies to all employers and the self-employed and covers everyone at work (including those on work experience and similar schemes) and non-workers, such as visitors, affected by the work.

All accidents, diseases and dangerous occurrences can now be reported to a single point:

**Incident Contact Centre (ICC),
Caerphilly Business Park,
Caerphilly CF83 3GG.**

You can report incidents:

- by telephone between 8.30 am and 5.00 pm Monday to Friday on **0845 300 9923** (charged at local call rate);
- by fax on **0845 300 9924** (charged at local call rate);
- via the Internet at **www.riddor.gov.uk** or **www.hse.gov.uk**;
- by e-mail to **riddor@natbrit.com**; or
- by post to the ICC at Caerphilly.

Keep details of the incident, eg in your accident book.

You must notify the ICC:

- immediately of a death or major injury, such as a broken arm or leg, an amputation injury or where an employee or the self-employed person is seriously affected by, eg electric shock or poisoning, or where a member of the public is killed or taken to hospital;
- immediately of a dangerous occurrence, eg where something happens like a fire or explosion which stops work for more than 24 hours;
- within 10 days of an 'over-three-day injury', ie when an employee or self-employed person has an accident at work and is unable to do their normal job for more than three days;
- as soon as possible of a work-related disease (as specified in RIDDOR);
- immediately, if you supply, fill or import liquefied petroleum gas (LPG) in refillable containers, of any death or major injury connected in any way with this LPG and confirm the notification within 14 days.

What to do when there is an accident

- Take any action required to deal with the immediate risks, eg first aid, put out the fire, isolate any danger, fence off the area.
- Assess the amount and kind of investigation needed – if you have to disturb the site, take photographs and measurements first.
- Investigate – find out what happened and why.
- Take steps to stop something similar happening again.
- Also look at near misses and property damage. Often it is only by chance that someone wasn't injured.

Checklist

Don't just focus on individuals and the immediate causes, look also at how the job, the work environment and the organisation may have contributed.

To help with your investigation, find out the following:

- Details of injured personnel.
- Details of injury, damage or loss.
- What was the worst that could have happened?
- Could it happen again?
- What happened? Where? When?
- What was the direct cause?
- Were there standards in place for the premises, plant, substances, procedures involved?
- Were they adequate? Were they followed?
- Were the people up to the job?
- Were they competent, trained and instructed?
- What was the underlying cause? Was there more than one?
- What was meant to happen and what were the plans?
- How were the people organised?
- Would inspection would have picked up the problem earlier?
- Had it happened before? If so, why weren't the lessons learnt?

25 Accidents and emergencies

First aid

You need to assess your first-aid requirements to help you decide what equipment, facilities and personnel you should provide.

The minimum first-aid provision at any workplace is:

■ a suitably stocked first-aid box;
■ an appointed person to take charge of first-aid arrangements.

Put up notices telling your employees:

■ who and where the first-aiders or appointed persons are;
■ where the first-aid box is.

You may need more than the minimum provision, including trained first-aiders. The number of first-aiders required will depend on the outcome of your first-aid needs assessment.

Your assessment may also indicate you should provide a first-aid room, particularly where your work involves certain hazards such as those that may be found in chemical industries and large construction sites.

As your company grows, look again at your need for qualified first-aiders. They must have the right training and are given a certificate valid for three years – after that a refresher course and re-examination is necessary. Training organisations are approved by HSE – contact HSE's Infoline for details.

Find out more

A guide to the Reporting of Injuries, Diseases and Dangerous Occurrences Regulations 1995 L73 (Second edition) ISBN 0 7176 2431 5

First aid at work. The Health and Safety (First Aid) Regulations 1981. Approved Code of Practice and guidance L74 ISBN 0 7176 1050 0

Investigating accidents and incidents: A workbook for employers, unions, safety representatives and safety professionals HSG245 ISBN 0 7176 2827 2

Basic advice on first aid at work Poster ISBN 0 7176 6195 4

RIDDOR explained: Reporting of Injuries, Diseases and Dangerous Occurrences Regulations Leaflet HSE31(rev1)

First aid at work: Your questions answered Leaflet INDG214

Basic advice on first aid at work Leaflet INDG347(rev1)

Useful contacts

HSE Infoline
Caerphilly Business Park, Caerphilly CF83 3GG Tel: 0845 345 0055
Textphone: 0845 408 9577 e-mail: hse.infoline@natbrit.com
Website: www.hse.gov.uk/contact/ask.htm

HSE Books
HSE Books, PO Box 1999, Sudbury, Suffolk CO10 2WA Tel: 01787 881165
Fax: 01787 313995 Website: www.hsebooks.co.uk

Incident Contact Centre (ICC)
Caerphilly Business Park, Caerphilly CF83 3GG. Tel: 0845 300 9923
Fax: 0845 300 9924 e-mail: riddor@natbrit.com
Website: www.riddor.gov.uk or www.hse.gov.uk

British Safety Council
70 Chancellors Road, London W6 9RS Tel: 020 8741 1231
Website: www.britsafe.org

Confederation of British Industry
Centre Point,103 New Oxford Street, London WC1A 1DU Tel: 020 7395 8247
Website: www.cbi.org.uk

The Royal Society for the Prevention of Accidents (RoSPA)
Edgbaston Park, 353 Bristol Road, Edgbaston, Birmingham B5 7ST Tel: 0121 248 2000
Website: www.rospa.org.uk

Trades Union Congress
Congress House, Great Russell Street, London WC1B 3LS Tel: 020 7636 4030
Website: www.tuc.org.uk

Websites

HSE Small business web pages
www.hse.gov.uk/smallbusinesses/index.htm

HSE Business Benefits case studies
www.hse.gov.uk/businessbenefits/index.htm

Businesslink
Practical advice for businesses Tel: 0845 600 9006
www.businesslink.gov.uk

Environment Agency websites
www.environment-agency.gov.uk

www.netregs.gov.uk provides plain language guidance for small businesses on
environmental legislation and how to comply with it

Essentials of health and safety at work

HSE Infoline 0845 345 0055 HSE website www.hse.gov.uk HSE Books 01787 881165

Index

HSE Infoline 0845 345 0055 **HSE website** www.hse.gov.uk **HSE Books** 01787 881165

HSE Infoline 0845 345 0055 HSE website www.hse.gov.uk HSE Books 01787 881165

HSE Infoline 0845 345 0055 HSE website www.hse.gov.uk HSE Books 01787 881165

Printed and published by the Health and Safety Executive   C750   04/06

HSE Infoline 0845 345 0055 HSE website www.hse.gov.uk HSE Books 01787 881165